Vol. 1: Adult Beginners

CD Included

T0051158

Piano *Plain and Simple!*™

Reading ♦ Playing ♦ Creating
in all keys...*plus*...Theory Basics

Cynthia Pace

Cover Design: Robert Clancy

Signed Illustrations: Jeanne Benas

R Lee Roberts Music Publications, Inc.

Copyright ©1997 by Cynthia Pace
International Copyright Secured.
All Rights Reserved.

www.leerobertsmusic.com

Contents

Welcome!

About This Book

PIANO—PLAIN AND SIMPLE! offers adult beginners the excitement of playing and creating music, right from the very start. Here are some of the special advantages of this all-inclusive guide:

➤ **An outstanding selection of traditional and original compositions** provides students with many enjoyable opportunities for practicing and mastering skills needed for playing the piano. Upon completing this book, students will have gained a solid grounding in the fundamentals of CHORDING, TRANSPOSING, PLAYING EXPRESSIVELY, using the PEDAL, NOTATING MUSIC, and much more!

➤ **Plain and simple explanations** ensure that new concepts are easy to understand.

➤ **Clearly presented theory principles** aid students in learning new music more quickly.

➤ **Carefully designed writing exercises** help students remember important information more easily.

➤ **An early presentation of the black keys** along with the white keys broadens the range of music available to beginners, since, from the outset of this course, students become comfortable playing in all keys.

➤ **Step-by-step instructions for improvising and composing** introduce students to the endless rewards of creating their own music.

With *PIANO—PLAIN AND SIMPLE!* students enjoy a sense of continuous accomplishment, because the learning-level advances steadily but always well within reach. All in all, *PIANO—PLAIN AND SIMPLE!* is a beginner-friendly guide to the keyboard that makes learning fun, comprehensive, and lasting.

Study Hints

➤ **Practice regularly.** A half hour of practice three to five days each week will help you progress steadily.

➤ **Build on your abilities.** Always listen for what you like, as well as for what you want to improve, as you practice.

Happy Musical Adventures!

Sitting at the Piano

> ➤ SIT at the center of the keyboard.
>
> ➤ ADJUST the bench height so that your forearms, wrists, and hands form a line parallel to the floor.
>
> ➤ PLACE your feet on the floor near the pedals. One foot may be slightly in front of the other.

Hand Position

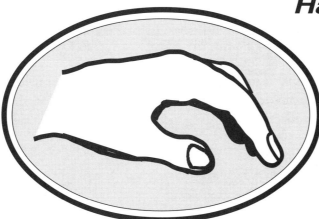

ROUND your hands so you can play on your fingertips and the outer corners of your thumbs.

5

Keyboard Basics

On this and the next page we will explore some important musical basics and will also prepare for improvising at the keyboard. As you follow the instructions below, temporarily "forget" what you may already know about scales, proper hand positions, or other musical patterns. Be adventurous! Play notes in any order, using any fingers you wish. The object here is to acquaint yourself with the wide range of sounds and effects your keyboard can create.

1 Start with any key and play several different keys. Begin softly, or "PIANO," and gradually get loud, or "FORTE," as you play. Use any finger(s).

Piano
(soft)

Forte
(loud)

> **LOUD and SOFT DYNAMIC contrast is very important in music.**

2 Play a series of any keys s-l-o-w-l-y, and another series fast. ALTERNATE speeds while playing a series of keys.

> **Like words in spoken languages, musical sounds come in many different combinations of lengths, or RHYTHMS.**

3 Play various keys: Release each key quickly before playing the next one. This creates short, STACCATO tones.

Now, play a series of sustained tones. Hold each key down until you play the next new key. This is LEGATO playing.

> **In music, SOUND is combined with SILENCE in a wide variety of ways.**

6

4 Hold the left SOFT PEDAL down with your left foot as you play several keys. (Keep your HEEL on the FLOOR).

Release the soft pedal. Now, hold the right DAMPER PEDAL with your right foot as you play a number of keys.

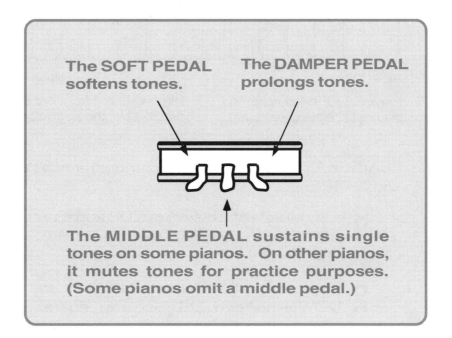

The SOFT PEDAL softens tones.

The DAMPER PEDAL prolongs tones.

The MIDDLE PEDAL sustains single tones on some pianos. On other pianos, it mutes tones for practice purposes. (Some pianos omit a middle pedal.)

5 Imagine a particular FEELING as you play. Can you play "enthusiastically?" "Reluctantly?" "Calmly?" "Sadly?" "Playfully?" Try expressing various moods by mixing dynamics, speed, touch (staccato/legato) and pedaling in various ways.

Blending your own FEELINGS with the MECHANICS of playing helps music convey many different emotions and ideas.

The Black Keys

Piano music can use the WHITE keys only, the BLACK keys only, or a combination of WHITE and BLACK keys. We'll begin with the black keys.

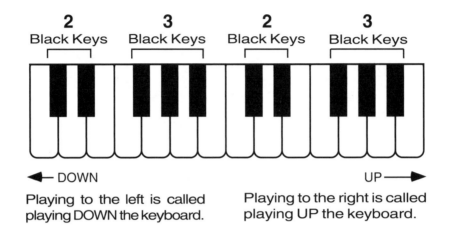

| 2 | 3 | 2 | 3 |
| Black Keys | Black Keys | Black Keys | Black Keys |

◄— DOWN   UP —►

Playing to the left is called playing DOWN the keyboard.

Playing to the right is called playing UP the keyboard.

BLACK KEYS appear in alternating sets of TWO and THREE.

1 Play all sets of 2 black keys UP and then back DOWN the keyboard. Use any fingers to do this.

2 Play all sets of 3 black keys UP and then DOWN the keyboard. Use any fingers.

Grouping two and three black keys together forms a PENTATONIC SCALE. Much music, including the songs you'll learn in the next chapter, uses the tones of the pentatonic scale.

Finger Numbers

The fingers on each hand are numbered 1 to 5, beginning with the thumb.

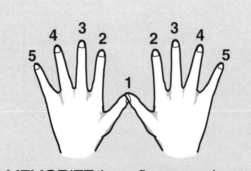

MEMORIZE these finger numbers.

Right Hand Up and Down

Pentatonic Scale

1 **1** Position the fingers of your RIGHT HAND on these black keys. Fingers 1, 2, and 3 go on a set of THREE black keys. Fingers 4 and 5 go on a set of TWO black keys. Follow the finger numbers in the notes below and play UP and back DOWN.

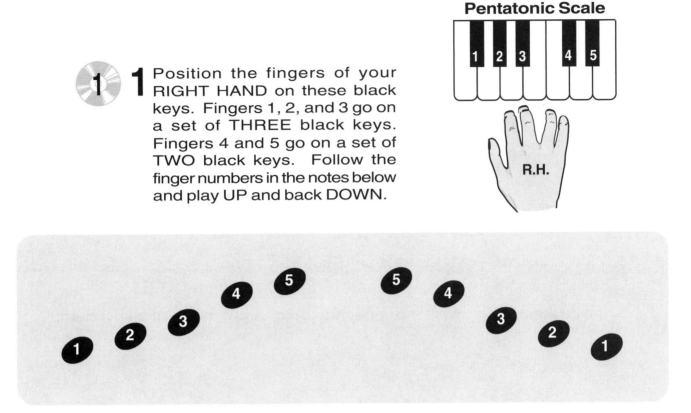

Left Hand Up and Down

Pentatonic Scale

2 **2** Position the fingers of your LEFT HAND on these black keys. Fingers 5, 4, and 3 go on a set of THREE black keys. Fingers 2 and 1 go on a set of TWO black keys. Follow the finger numbers in the notes below, and play UP and back DOWN.

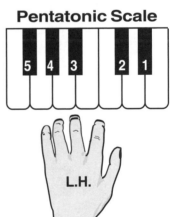

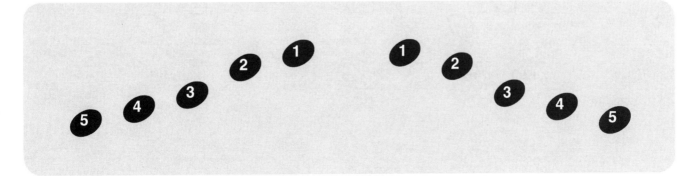

9

Review
(Pages 5 - 9)

1. The musical term "PIANO" means _____.

2. The musical term "FORTE" means _____.

3. Smooth playing is called "L _ _ _ _ _."

4. Short, detached sounds are called "S _ _ _ _ _ _ _."

5. When playing DOWN the keyboard, you play to the _____.
   (left or right)

6. Inside these notes, write the finger numbers for playing UP the keyboard.

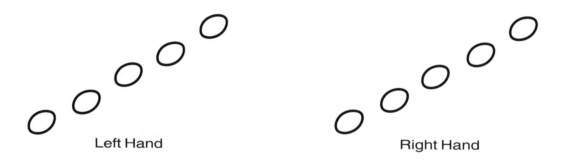

Left Hand   Right Hand

7. Write the finger numbers for playing DOWN the keyboard.

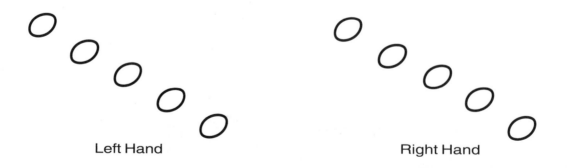

Left Hand   Right Hand

10

Note Reading

Notes are written in a left-to-right direction. While going across the page, notes may also move UPWARD or DOWNWARD. As you learn to read music, you will discover these principles:

UP-moving notes mean play to the **right.**

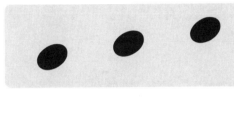
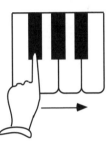

DOWN-moving notes mean play to the **left.**

Notes like this mean **REPEAT.**

(Play same note 3 times).

11

1 SAY the words to *Oh, Susanna!* as you CLAP along with them.

2 Place your LEFT HAND (L.H.) on the keyboard lid or other flat surface. Move the fingers indicated by the numbered notes below, saying or singing the finger numbers as you "play."

3 Position your LEFT HAND (L.H.) on the KEYBOARD and PRACTICE *Oh, Susanna!* As you play, hum the melody or sing the words.

DARK notes (●) represent quicker words. OPEN notes (○) represent words that hold longer.

OH, SUSANNA! 4

Stephen Foster

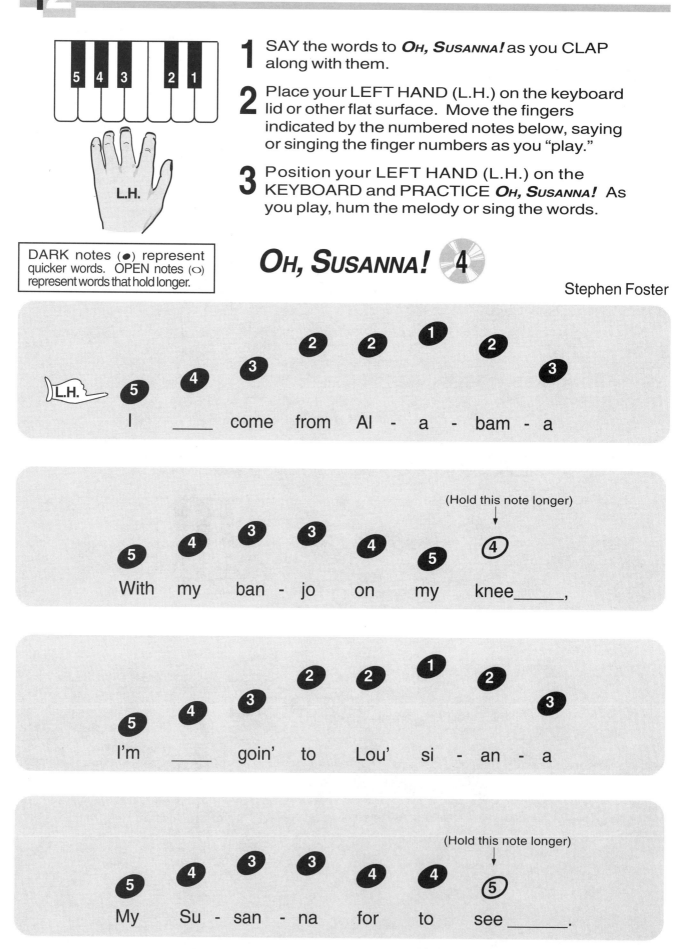

Practice *OH, SUSANNA!* with your RIGHT HAND. Use the same procedure as you did for your left hand on page 12.

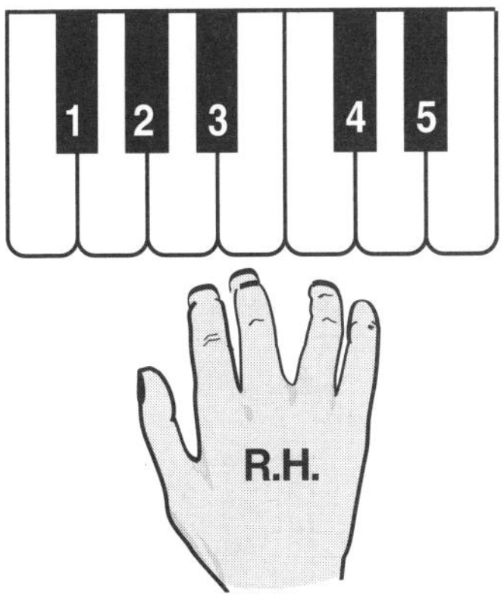

OH, SUSANNA! **4** *Cont'd*

Stephen Foster

R.H. ① ② ③ ④ ④ ⑤ ④ ③

It ___ rained all night the day I

① ② ③ ③ ② ① ②

(Hold this note longer)

left, the weath - er it was dry,

① ② ③ ④ ④ ⑤ ④ ③

The ___ sun so hot I froze to

(Hold this note longer)

① ② ③ ③ ② ② ①

death, Su - san - na don't you cry!

2364

Use this new position to play
THAT'S WHERE MY MONEY GOES.

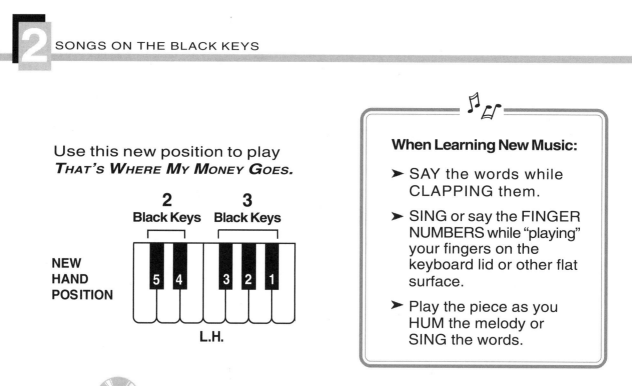

NEW HAND POSITION

When Learning New Music:

➤ SAY the words while CLAPPING them.

➤ SING or say the FINGER NUMBERS while "playing" your fingers on the keyboard lid or other flat surface.

➤ Play the piece as you HUM the melody or SING the words.

5 *THAT'S WHERE MY MONEY GOES*

American College Song

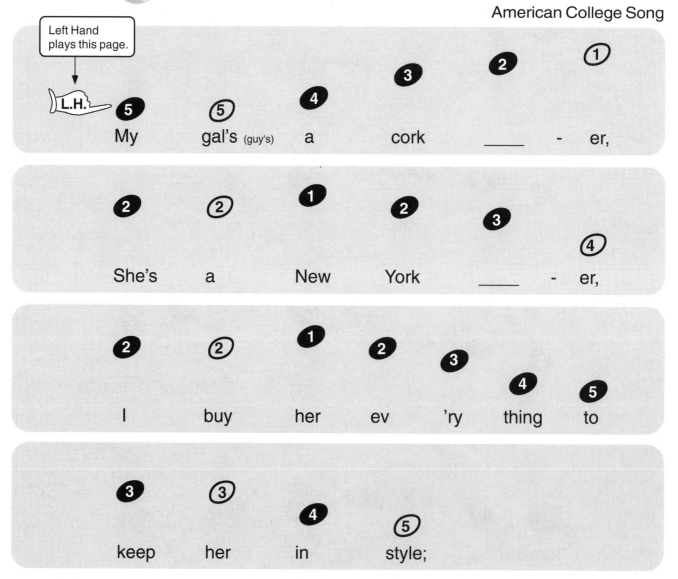

Left Hand plays this page.

My   gal's (guy's) a   cork ____ - er,

She's a   New   York ____ - er,

I   buy   her   ev   'ry   thing   to

keep   her   in   style;

On this page, continue *THAT'S WHERE MY MONEY GOES* with your RIGHT HAND.

2
Black Keys

3
Black Keys

NEW
HAND
POSITION

R.H.

5 Cont'd *THAT'S WHERE MY MONEY GOES*

American College Song

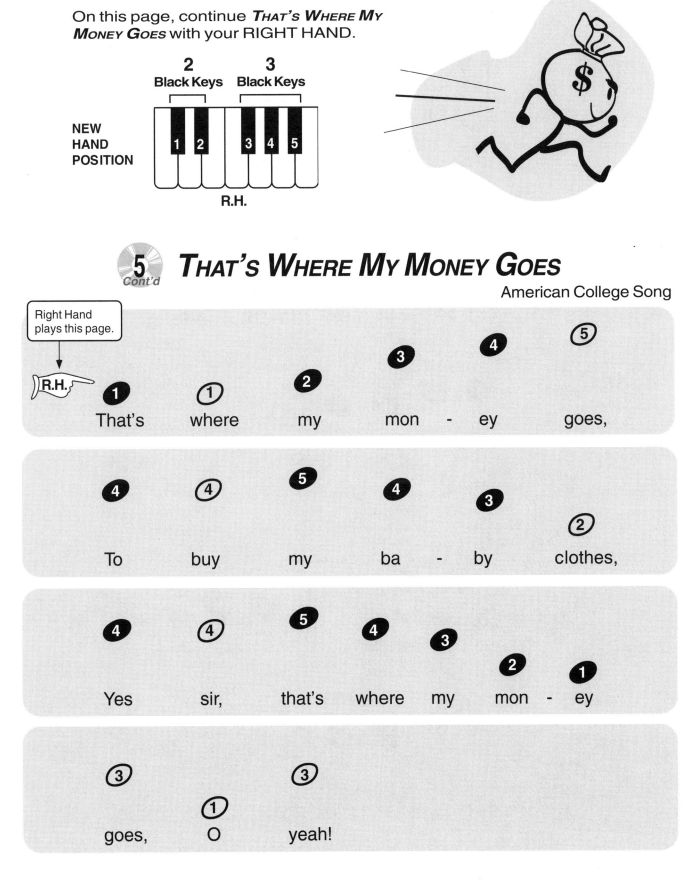

Right Hand plays this page.

R.H.

That's where my mon - ey goes,

To buy my ba - by clothes,

Yes sir, that's where my mon - ey

goes, O yeah!

15

In *OLD MACDONALD,* your RIGHT HAND plays lines 1 and 2. Your LEFT HAND follows, with lines 3 and 4.

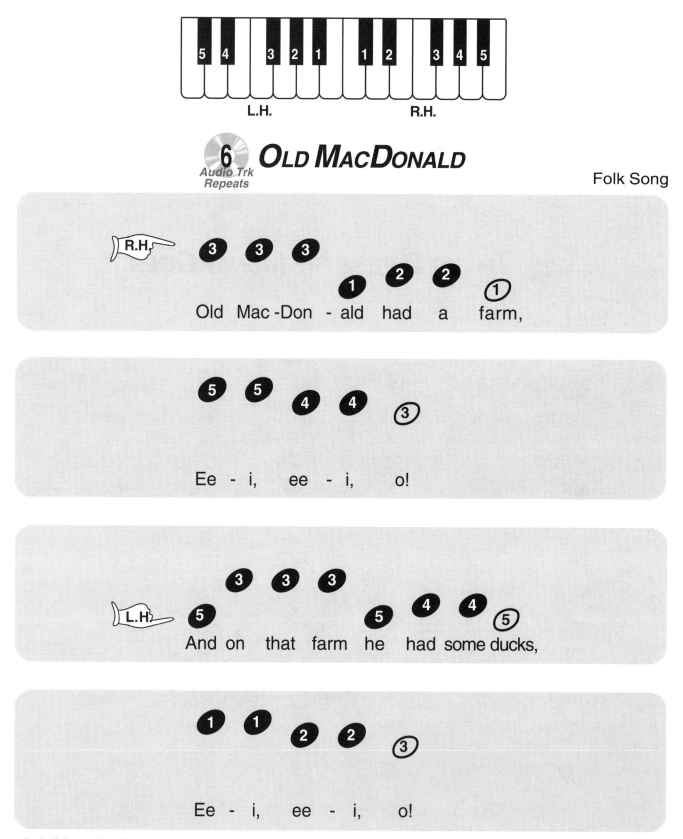

6 *OLD MACDONALD*

Audio Trk Repeats

Folk Song

Old Mac -Don - ald had a farm,

Ee - i, ee - i, o!

R.H.

L.H.
And on that farm he had some ducks,

Ee - i, ee - i, o!

Additional: See if you can discover how to play the remaining part of *OLD MACDONALD.*

MERRILY WE ROLL ALONG *does not* use left hand finger 2 or right hand finger 4. Rest these two fingers on the nearby white keys as you play.

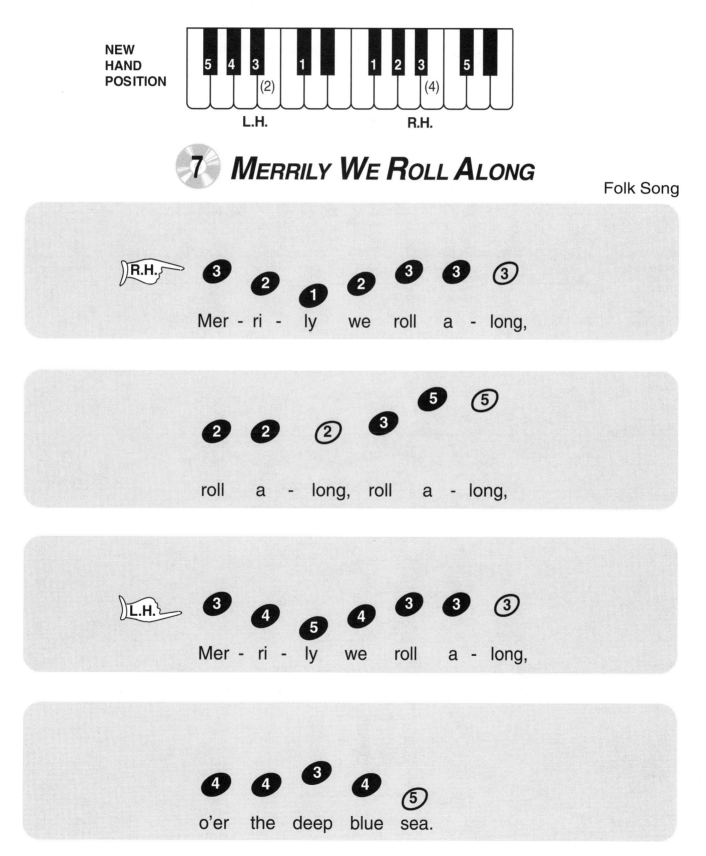

7 **MERRILY WE ROLL ALONG**

Folk Song

Creating Your Own Melodies

 **New Melodies**

You can create new melodies by playing DIFFERENT TONES along with a song's REGULAR WORDS.

1 POSITION your hands on these black keys:

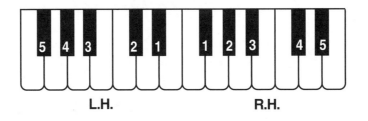

L.H.   **R.H.**

2 PLAY any of these keys (in any order) in time to the words for *OH SUSANNA!* Say the words as you play. Try one hand, then the other.

8
Audio Trk Repeats

OH, SUSANNA!

I___ come from Alabama
With my banjo on my knee,
I'm___ goin' to Lou'siana
My Susanna for to see.

3 END each new melody on this key, to make your song sound like it is "complete."

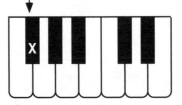

Additional: Use the words from other songs you know to create new melodies on the black keys.

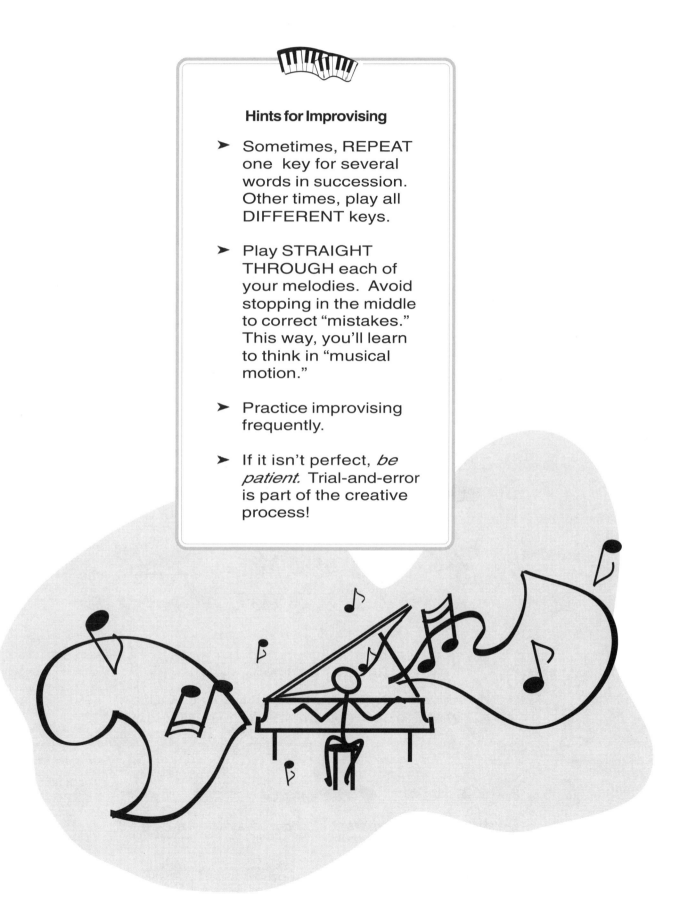

Hints for Improvising

➤ Sometimes, REPEAT one key for several words in succession. Other times, play all DIFFERENT keys.

➤ Play STRAIGHT THROUGH each of your melodies. Avoid stopping in the middle to correct "mistakes." This way, you'll learn to think in "musical motion."

➤ Practice improvising frequently.

➤ If it isn't perfect, *be patient.* Trial-and-error is part of the creative process!

3

Quarter and Half Notes

QUARTER NOTE

1 Beat

NOTES (♩, ♪) tell you HOW LONG to hold a tone. Different kinds of notes are held for different lengths of time. The LENGTH OF TIME a particular note is held is measured in units called BEATS. Beats are pulses. A beat is often represented by a foot tap.

HALF NOTE

2 Beats

Keeping Track of the Timing

To keep track of the timing, or RHYTHM, of notes:

1 Tap your foot steadily. Play or clap the notes, holding each note for the number of foot taps, or BEATS, it should get:

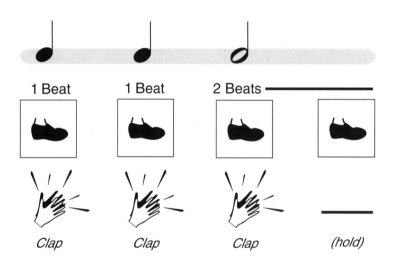

|1 Beat|1 Beat|2 Beats ——————|
|Clap|Clap|Clap|(hold)|

2 As you play (or clap), COUNT OUT LOUD by saying each note's name RHYTHMICALLY:

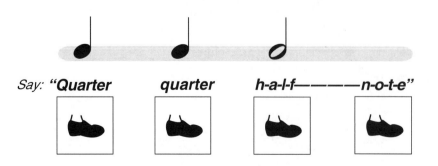

Say: **"Quarter**   **quarter**   **h-a-l-f————n-o-t-e"**

Playing Songs While Counting

1 CLAP the rhythm to this excerpt from
HOT CROSS BUNS as you say "quarter"
and "half-note."

2 PLAY *HOT CROSS BUNS* as shown.
Then, practice counting (saying) each
note's RHYTHMIC NAME as you play.

 **9** ## HOT CROSS BUNS

Folk Song

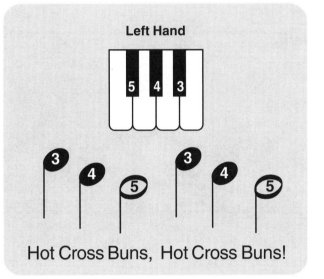

Hot Cross Buns, Hot Cross Buns!

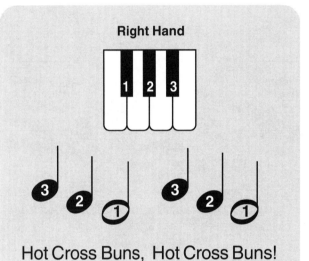

Hot Cross Buns, Hot Cross Buns!

Counting Practice

CLAP these notes as you SAY their RHYTHMIC NAMES. Then,
play these rhythms on any black keys.

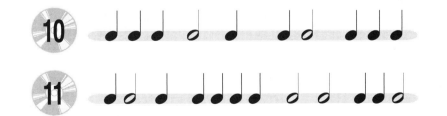

Create your own rhythmic pattern by writing some quarter and
half notes on the line below. CLAP your notes as you say their
rhythmic names. Play your rhythm on any black keys.

21

Transposing to the White Keys

For variety, the same music is often played in many different places on the keyboard. We call this "TRANSPOSING."

TRANSPOSE *HOT CROSS BUNS* by playing it on the three NEW sets of WHITE KEYS shown below.

HOT CROSS BUNS
(Finger Pattern)

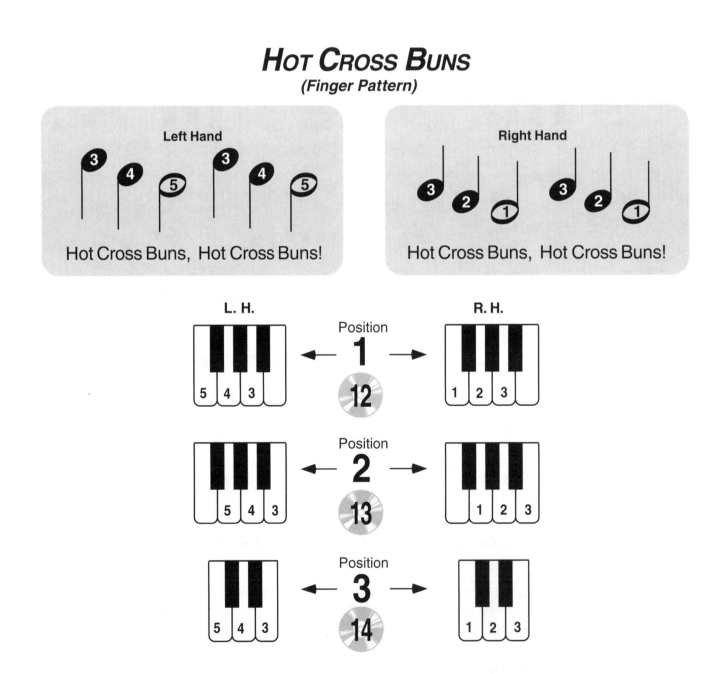

2364

Naming The White Keys

The WHITE KEYS, or "NATURAL KEYS," are named with the seven letters A - G, repeated over and over. Standard piano keyboards begin with A and end with C. Smaller keyboards sometimes begin with C.

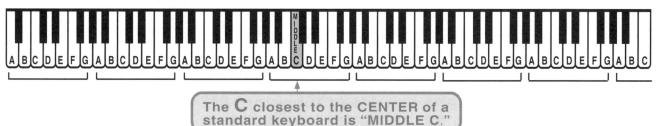

The **C** closest to the **CENTER** of a standard keyboard is "MIDDLE C."

You can recognize each white key by its neighboring black keys.

D lies between TWO black keys. G and A lie between THREE black keys.

C and E lie just outside TWO black keys. F and B lie just outside three black keys.

Learning Suggestions:

1 PLAY and NAME all the white keys from left to right.

2 Identify the white keys located BETWEEN the black keys: Play all D's, then all G's and all A's. Then, identify the white keys located OUTSIDE the black keys: Play all C's, all E's, all F's, and all B's.

3 NAME and PLAY individual white keys in various orders a few times each day until you can quickly identify any key.

The C Major Tune-up

A MAJOR TUNE-UP is a set of five keys lying next to one another, as shown below. Many melodies are based on this simple pattern.

1 POSITION your fingers on the keys of a C major tune-up, shown here.

C Major Tune-up

L.H.   R.H.

2 One hand at a time, PLAY UP and DOWN a C major tune-up, as the notes below indicate. SING each letter name as you play.

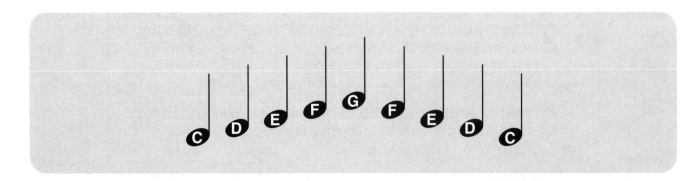

C D E F G F E D C

Practice *TUNE-UP EXERCISE NO. 1* hands alone and, later, hands together. Sing each letter-name as you play. Keep a rounded hand position; relaxed, flexible wrist; and curved fingers.

C Major Tune-up

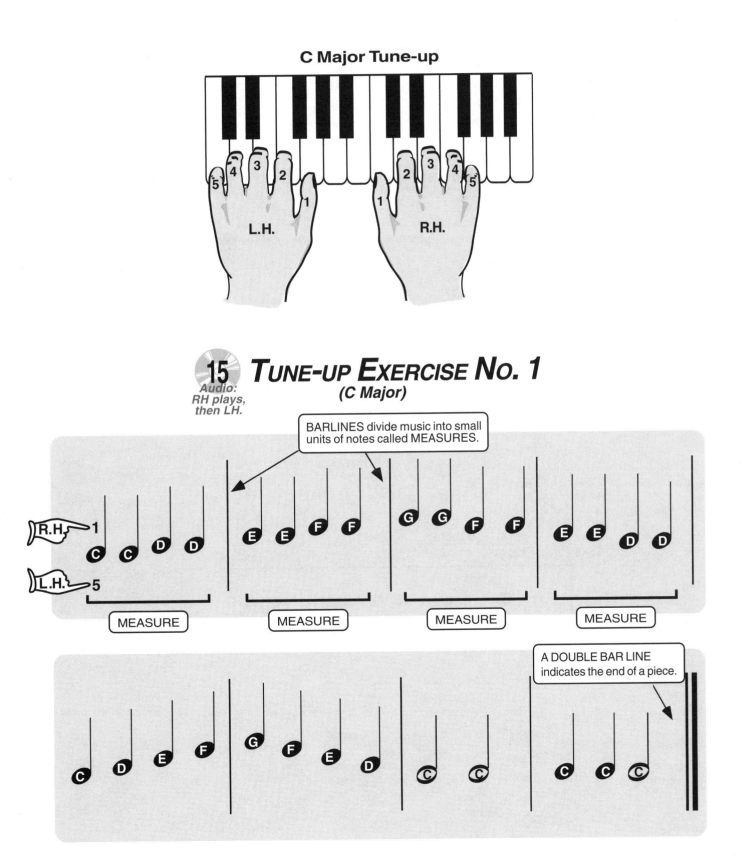

15 Audio: *RH plays, then LH.*

TUNE-UP EXERCISE NO. 1
(C Major)

BARLINES divide music into small units of notes called MEASURES.

A DOUBLE BAR LINE indicates the end of a piece.

Repeating Notes

Finding patterns or RELATIONSHIPS in the music you play will help you learn and remember new pieces more easily. Often, patterns are created by consecutive repeating notes.

REPEATING NOTES: Note plays **again.**

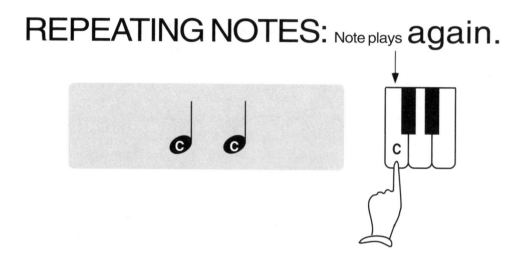

Circle the REPEATING NOTES in *THEME FROM THE NINTH,* page 27.

1 Position your fingers on a C MAJOR TUNE-UP and practice *THEME FROM THE NINTH* in one hand, then in the other hand.

2 After you've learned *THEME FROM THE NINTH* hands separately, try both hands together.

C Major Tune-up

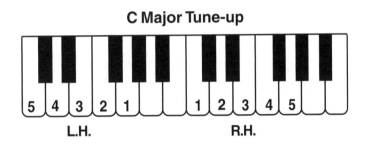

L.H.   R.H.

16 # THEME FROM THE NINTH SYMPHONY
(C Major)

Beethoven

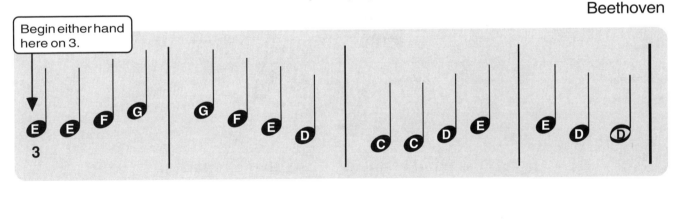

Begin either hand here on 3.

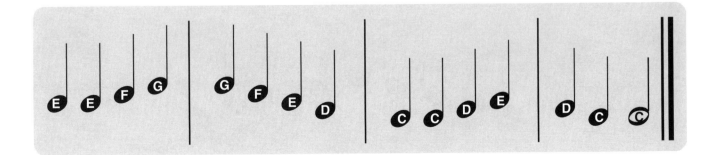

27

The G Major Tune-up

1 POSITION your fingers on the keys of a G major tune-up, as shown.

G Major Tune-up

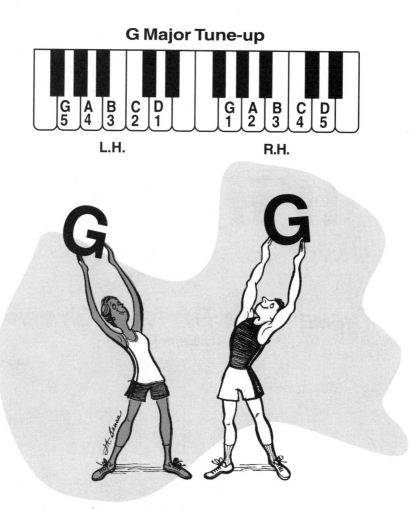

L.H.   R.H.

2 One hand at a time, PLAY these notes up and down the G major tune-up. SING each letter name as you play.

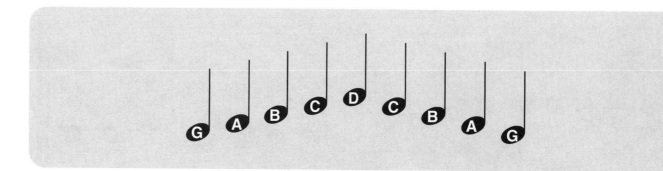

Practice *TUNE-UP EXERCISE NO. 1* in G major, hands alone and, then, hands together. Sing each letter-name as you play. Keep a rounded hand position; relaxed, flexible wrist; and curved fingers.

G Major Tune-up

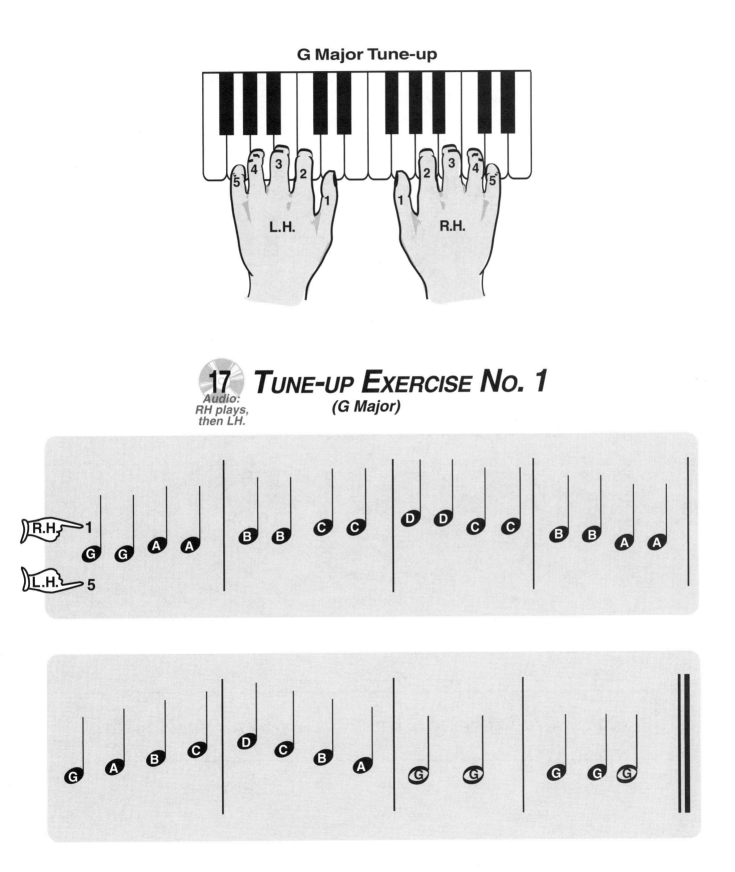

17 *Audio: RH plays, then LH.*

TUNE-UP EXERCISE NO. 1
(G Major)

Stepping Notes

Neighboring notes ONE LETTER NAME apart are called STEPPING NOTES.

UPWARD STEP: Play to the right.

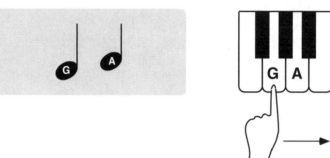

DOWNWARD STEP: Play to the left.

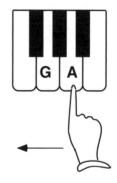

✍ Circle the STEPPING NOTES in *THEME FROM THE NINTH,* page 31.

1 Position your fingers on a G MAJOR TUNE-UP and practice *THEME FROM THE NINTH* in one hand, then in the other hand.

2 After you've learned *THEME FROM THE NINTH* hands separately, try both hands together.

G Major Tune-up

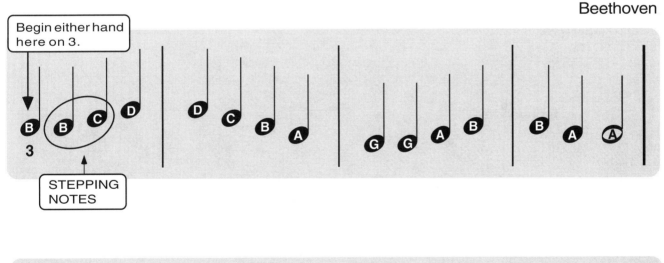

L.H.   R.H.

18 THEME FROM THE NINTH SYMPHONY
(G Major)

Beethoven

Begin either hand here on 3.

B 3 B C D   D C B A   G G A B   B A A

STEPPING NOTES

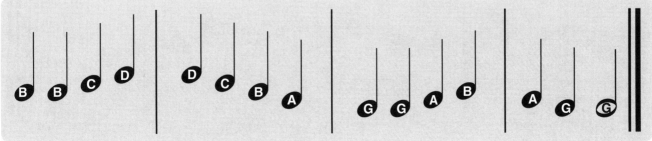

B B C D   D C B A   G G A B   A G G

2364

Skipping Notes

Notes SEPARATED by ONE OR MORE LETTER NAMES are called SKIPPING NOTES.

SKIP UP

SKIP DOWN

Circle the SKIPPING NOTES in *LOVE SOMEBODY,* then practice this piece.

C Major Tune-up

19 LOVE SOMEBODY
(C Major)

Folk Song

SKIPPING NOTES

R.H.

Love some - bod - y, yes I do! Love some- bod - y, won - der who?

L.H.

Love some-bod- y, deed I do! Won-der if - it could be you?

Transpose *LOVE SOMEBODY* to the G major tune-up position, as shown below.

G Major Tune-up

20 *LOVE SOMEBODY*
(G Major)

Folk Song

Love some-bod-y, yes I do! Love some-bod-y, won-der who?

Love some-bod-y, deed I do! Won-der if-it could be you?

Good Reading Habits

When first playing new music, keep your eyes on the page, not on your hands.

Review
(Pages 11 - 33)

1. A _____ note gets 1 beat. A _____ note gets 2 beats.

2. CLAP these notes as you COUNT "quarter" or "half note" rhythmically.
   PLAY this rhythm on any keys while counting aloud.

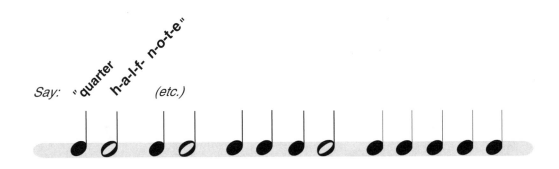

3. Write quarter and half notes on the lines below to create your own
   rhythmic patterns. CLAP your patterns while saying "quarter" or
   "half note." PLAY these on any keys.

4. Write "UP" or "DOWN" for the
   direction these notes move.

   _____   _____

5. Write "LEFT" or "RIGHT" for the
   direction you should play.

   _____   _____

2364

Lines and Spaces

Notes are written on LINES →
and
SPACES. →

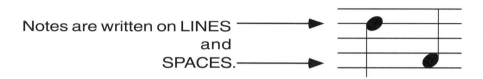

A set of 5 LINES and the SPACES between form a STAFF.

The Grand Staff

Piano music is notated on a pair of staves called the GRAND STAFF.

A TREBLE CLEF (𝄞)
identifies the top staff.

A BASS CLEF (𝄢)
identifies the bottom staff.

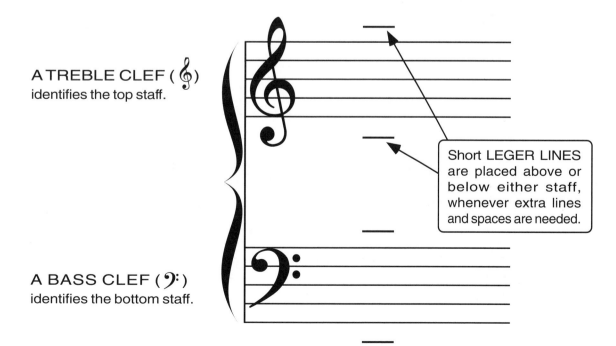

Short LEGER LINES are placed above or below either staff, whenever extra lines and spaces are needed.

The Keyboard and the Grand Staff

Each line and space of the Grand Staff corresponds to a piano key. (We'll begin with the WHITE KEYS and add the black keys soon).

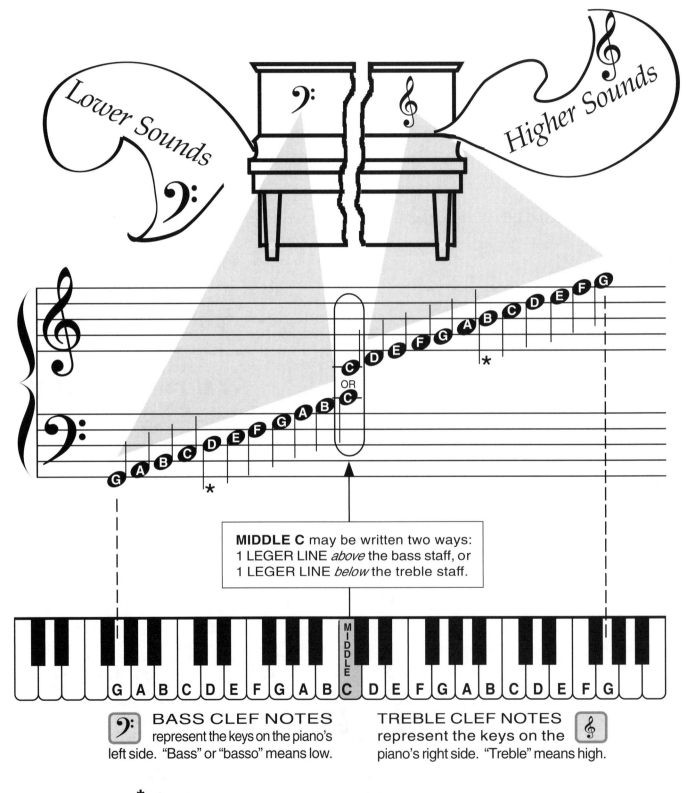

MIDDLE C may be written two ways:
1 LEGER LINE *above* the bass staff, or
1 LEGER LINE *below* the treble staff.

BASS CLEF NOTES represent the keys on the piano's left side. "Bass" or "basso" means low.

TREBLE CLEF NOTES represent the keys on the piano's right side. "Treble" means high.

*Notes above a staff's middle line are usually stemmed down (♩).

36

Low, Middle, and High Registers

The letters A - G appear on the GRAND STAFF three times, in a LOWER, MIDDLE, and HIGHER REGISTER.

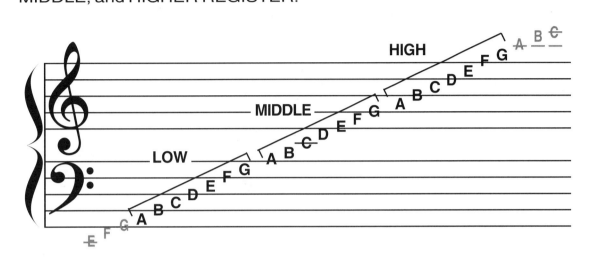

WRITE the letters A - G in their LOW, MIDDLE, and HIGH REGISTERS.

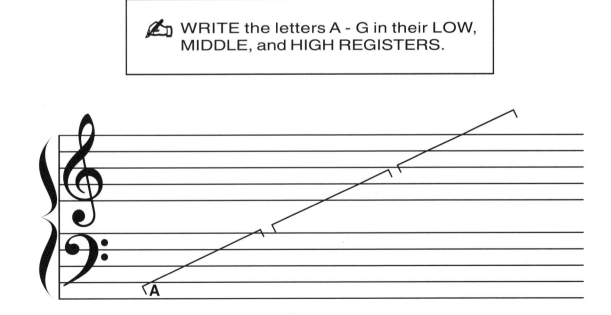

Playing In The Treble Clef

Your RIGHT HAND usually plays TREBLE CLEF notes.

Play these treble clef notes UP the keyboard with the second finger of your RIGHT HAND. Begin on Middle C and name each note as you play.

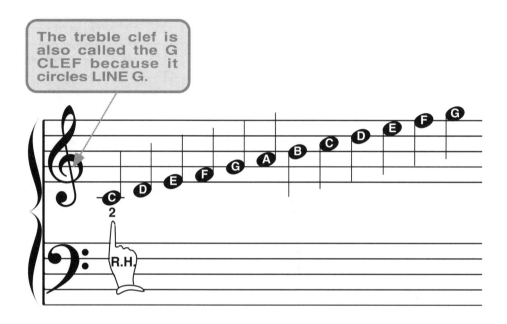

The treble clef is also called the G CLEF because it circles LINE G.

Time Signatures

A TIME SIGNATURE is a pair of numbers at the beginning of a piece.

The top number tells HOW MANY BEATS are in each measure.

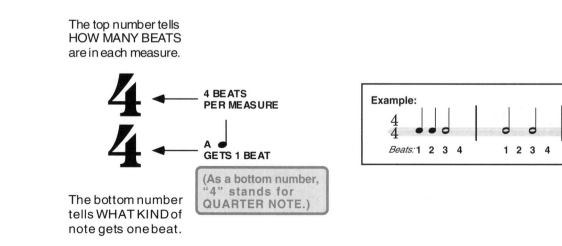

4 ← 4 BEATS PER MEASURE

4 ← A ♩ GETS 1 BEAT

(As a bottom number, "4" stands for QUARTER NOTE.)

The bottom number tells WHAT KIND of note gets one beat.

Writing Practice

1. Draw three 𝄞's:

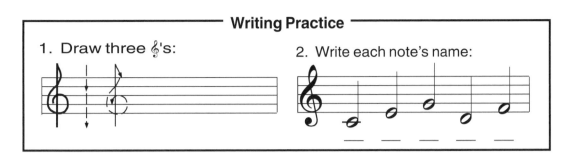

2. Write each note's name:

---

1 CLAP the rhythm of *FRERE JACQUES* while saying "quarter" or "half note." Next, SAY the LETTER-NAMES of the notes.

2 Position your RIGHT hand on this C major tune-up, then PLAY *FRERE JACQUES.* (The second half of this melody varies slightly from the usual version of the folk song). Sing the notes' letter-names the first few times you play.

C Major Tune-up (R.H.)

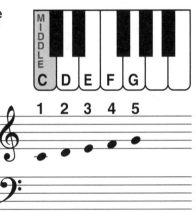

21 *FRERE JACQUES*
(Adapted)

French Folk Song

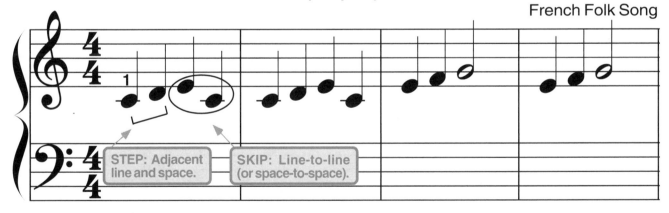

STEP: Adjacent line and space.

SKIP: Line-to-line (or space-to-space).

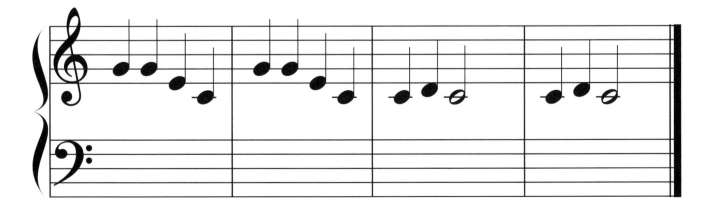

39

Writing Practice

Write each note's name:

f for FORTE:
play LOUDLY.

p for PIANO:
play SOFTLY.

G Major Tune-up (R.H.)

1 Notice that *FRERE JACQUES* is composed of PATTERNS and REPETITIONS of these patterns.

2 With your right hand, play this version of *FRERE JACQUES* in G major as shown. Follow the f and p dynamic indications, playing patterns loudly (f) and repetitions softly (p). Sing the notes' letter-names when you first play.

22 **FRERE JACQUES**
(G Major)

PATTERN   REPETITION   PATTERN   REPETITION *(etc.)*

Writing Practice

Below, in the blank treble clef measures, WRITE a REPETITION for each pattern.

C Major Tune-up (R.H.)

After completing the music below, name each note. Then, PLAY this version of *FRERE JACQUES* which begins on the C above Middle C.

23 *FRERE JACQUES*

PATTERN	REPETITION	PATTERN	REPETITION *(etc.)*

Stems point down on notes above middle line.

Additional: Reverse the dynamic scheme of page 40—play PATTERNS *p* and REPETITIONS *f*.

You and a partner find two different C major tune-up positions, then play *FRERE JACQUES* as a round.

41

Writing in the Treble Clef

1. Draw some TREBLE CLEFS:

2. Write the treble clef LINE-names C, E, G, B, D, and F:

3. Write the names of these LINE-notes:

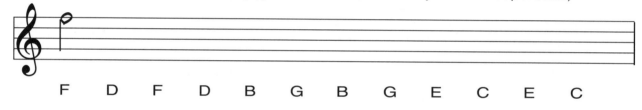

4. Write HALF NOTES on these LINES. (Notes above the middle line are stemmed down (♩).
   Notes below the middle line are stemmed up (♩). Notes on the middle line may be stemmed up or down.)

     F   D   F   D   B   G   B   G   E   C   E   C

5. Write the treble clef SPACE-names:

6. Write the names of these SPACE-notes:

7. Write HALF NOTES on these SPACES:

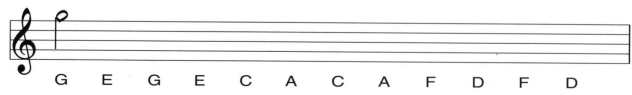

     G   E   G   E   C   A   C   A   F   D   F   D

Playing In The Bass Clef

Your LEFT HAND usually plays BASS CLEF notes.

Play these bass clef notes DOWN the keyboard with the second finger of your LEFT HAND. Begin on Middle C and name each note as you play.

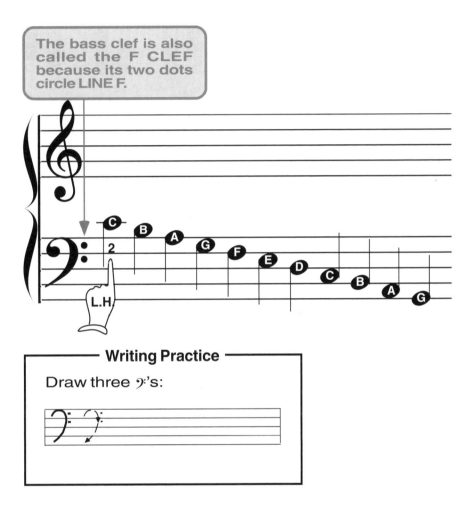

The bass clef is also called the F CLEF because its two dots circle LINE F.

Writing Practice

Draw three 𝄢's:

Time Signature Review

1. Add barlines below so that FOUR beats occur in each measure.

2. Add barlines below so that THREE beats occur in each measure.

43

Writing Practice

Write each note's name:

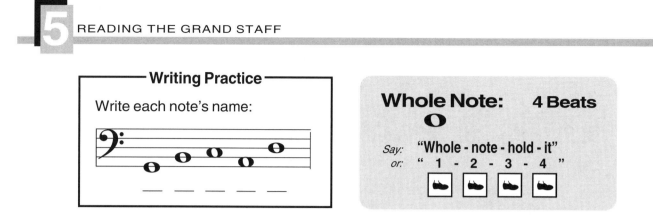

Whole Note: **4 Beats**

𝐨

Say: "Whole - note - hold - it"
or: " 1 - 2 - 3 - 4 "

1 Look for patterns that repeat in *THE CRESTED HEN.* CLAP the rhythm of this song while saying "half note," "quarter," and "whole-note-hold-it." SAY the LETTER-NAMES of the notes.

2 Position your LEFT hand, as shown, then play *THE CRESTED HEN.* Sing the notes' letter-names the first few times you play.

G Major Tune-up (L.H.)

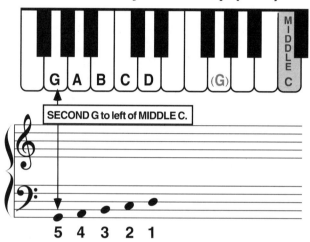

SECOND G to left of MIDDLE C.

5 4 3 2 1

24 *THE CRESTED HEN*

Danish Folk Song

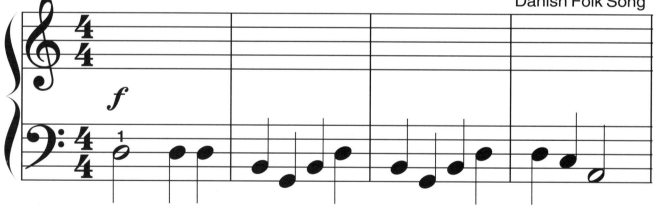

𝑓

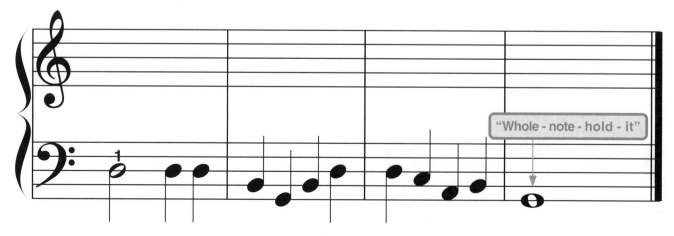

"Whole - note - hold - it"

44

Writing Practice

Write each note's name:

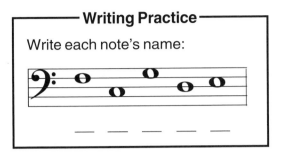

— — — — —

Rests:

Rests tell you where NOT to play.
They designate musical SILENCE.

Whole Measure Rest **=** **Silence for Entire Measure**

1 CLAP the rhythm while saying "half note" and "quarter." SAY the LETTER-NAMES of the notes.

C Major Tune-up (L.H.)

2 Position your LEFT hand on this C major tune-up, then play *HEY LOLLY.* Sing the notes' letter-names the first few times you play.

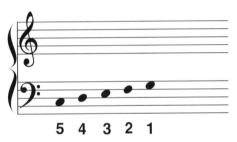

5 4 3 2 1

WHOLE MEASURE REST:
R.H. silent while L. H. plays.

25 *HEY LOLLY*

Folk Song

mf (MEZZO FORTE: Medium loud)

2364

In *NIGHT COMES BACK AGAIN,* your LEFT HAND begins in the BASS CLEF, then your RIGHT HAND continues in the TREBLE CLEF. At the end of this song, both hands play together.

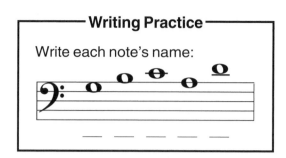

Writing Practice

Write each note's name:

1 CLAP the rhythm of *NIGHT COMES BACK* while saying "quarter," "half note," or "whole-note-hold-it." Then, SAY the LETTER-NAMES of the notes.

2 Position BOTH hands then play. (Notice that this song does not use the tone D).

G Major Tune-up

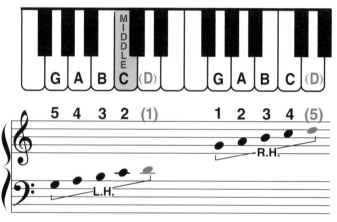

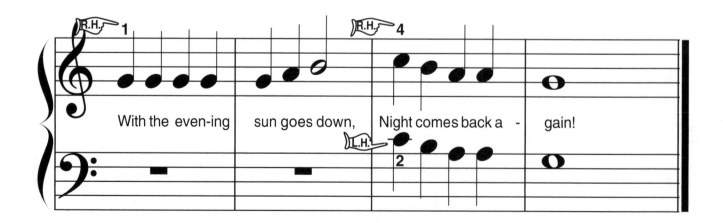

26 *NIGHT COMES BACK AGAIN*

Czeck Folk Song

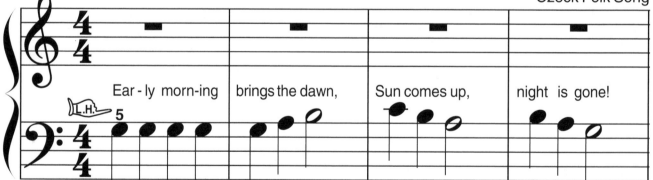

Ear - ly morn-ing | brings the dawn, | Sun comes up, | night is gone!

With the even-ing | sun goes down, | Night comes back a - | gain!

Writing in the Bass Clef

1. Draw several BASS CLEFS:

2. Write the bass clef LINE-names G, B, D, F, A, and C:

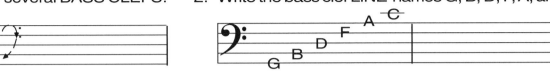

3. Write the names of these LINE-notes:

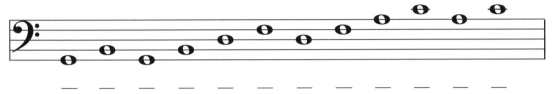

4. Write WHOLE NOTES on these LINES:

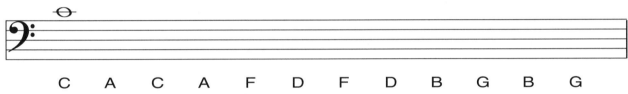

C   A   C   A   F   D   F   D   B   G   B   G

5. Write the bass clef SPACE-names:

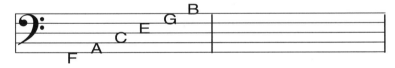

6. Write the names of these SPACE-notes:

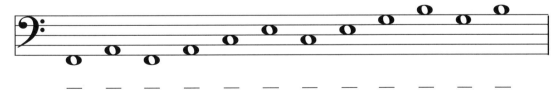

7. Write WHOLE NOTES on these SPACES:

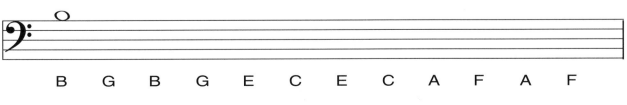

B   G   B   G   E   C   E   C   A   F   A   F

2364

Practicing With Flashcards

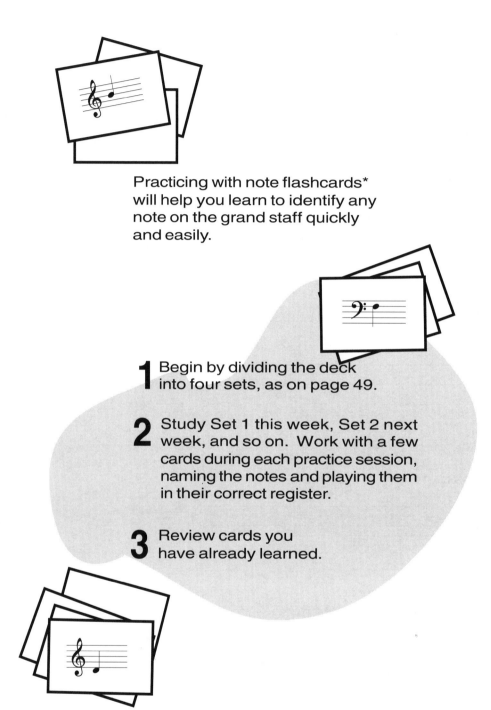

Practicing with note flashcards*
will help you learn to identify any
note on the grand staff quickly
and easily.

1 Begin by dividing the deck
into four sets, as on page 49.

2 Study Set 1 this week, Set 2 next
week, and so on. Work with a few
cards during each practice session,
naming the notes and playing them
in their correct register.

3 Review cards you
have already learned.

* Lines and Space Flashcards, © Lee Roberts Music Pub., Inc., are available through your music dealer.

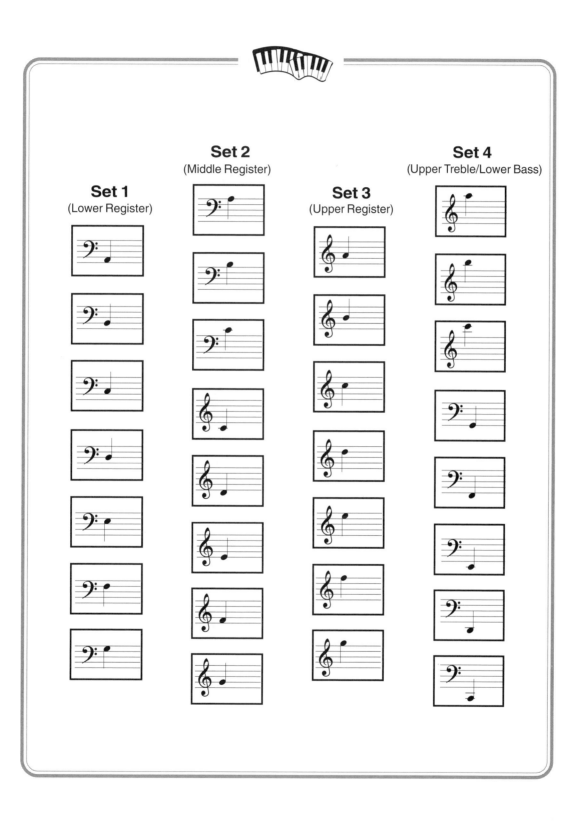

Set 1
(Lower Register)

Set 2
(Middle Register)

Set 3
(Upper Register)

Set 4
(Upper Treble/Lower Bass)

6

Flats

♭ Flats:

A flat before a note means play the VERY NEXT KEY to the LEFT.

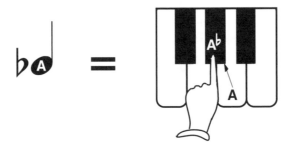

Notice that five flats are black keys while two flats are white keys. Play the five BLACK-KEY flats.

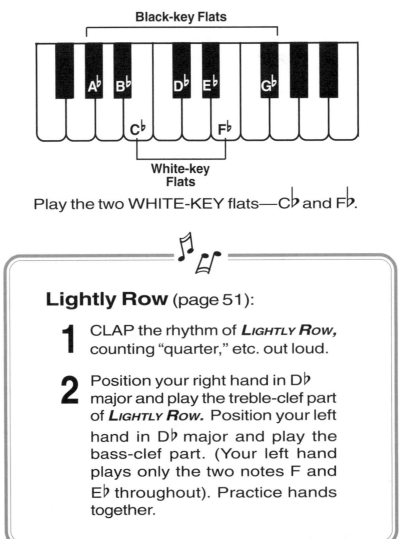

Play the two WHITE-KEY flats—C♭ and F♭.

Lightly Row (page 51):

1 CLAP the rhythm of *LIGHTLY ROW,* counting "quarter," etc. out loud.

2 Position your right hand in D♭ major and play the treble-clef part of *LIGHTLY ROW.* Position your left hand in D♭ major and play the bass-clef part. (Your left hand plays only the two notes F and E♭ throughout). Practice hands together.

D♭ Major Tune-up

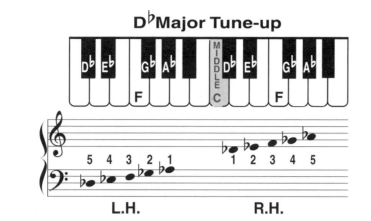

L.H.   R.H.

27 LIGHTLY ROW
(D♭ Major)

Folk Song

A FLAT applies to a given note for the ENTIRE measure and needs to be indicated only once per measure.

Sharps

♯ Sharps:

A sharp before a note means play the VERY NEXT KEY to the RIGHT.

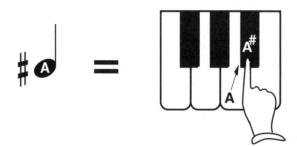

Notice that five sharps are black keys while two sharps are white keys. Play the five BLACK-KEY sharps.

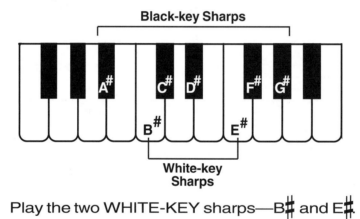

Play the two WHITE-KEY sharps—B♯ and E♯

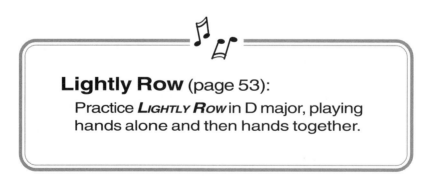

Lightly Row (page 53):

Practice *LIGHTLY ROW* in D major, playing hands alone and then hands together.

D Major Tune-up

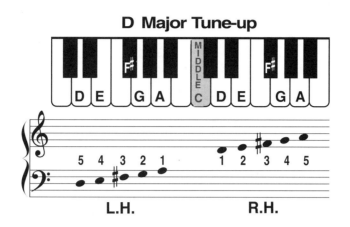

28 LIGHTLY ROW
(D Major)

Folk Song

A SHARP applies to a given note for the ENTIRE measure and needs to be indicated only once per measure.

Whole Steps and Half Steps

HALF STEP: Any key plus the **very next key**.
(No other keys between)

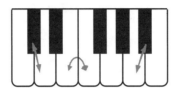

WHOLE STEP: Two keys with **one other key** between.

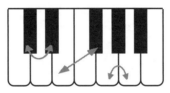

Alley Cat (page 55):

1 Clap the right hand part, saying "quarter," "half note," or "whole-note-hold-it."

2 Locate your right-hand position.

Hand Position: *ALLEY CAT*

L.H.   R.H.

Play the right hand part (page 55), following the fingering indicated above the notes. (R.H. fingers 5 and 4 do "double duty:" 5 begins with F and 4 follows with E. Later, at the end of line 1, finger 4 moves to D♯ and 5 moves to E.) *ALLEY CAT* is easy to learn because it proceeds mainly by half steps, going from one key to the next neighbor, and so on.

3 Play the left hand part alone. Notice that this part uses only two notes—F and C.

4 Play hands together.

54

Half Rest:  = Silence for 2 beats in $\frac{2}{4}$, $\frac{3}{4}$, or $\frac{4}{4}$ time.

Half rests (━) look like inverted whole measure rests (▬).

29 ALLEY CAT

Frank Bjorn, Music
Al Stillman, Words

He goes on the prowl each night like an Al - ley Cat,

Look-in for some new de - light like an Al - ley Cat.

Left Hand rests while Right Hand plays.

D♭ means the same key as C♯.

Finger 4 moves to D♯ and finger 5 moves to E.

Say: "Half rest" (or "1 - 2"). **Left hand plays after waiting 2 beats.**

Major Tune-ups

THEME FROM THE NINTH, LOVE SOMEBODY, LIGHTLY ROW and many other pieces are composed from a MAJOR TUNE-UP PATTERN.

Major Tune-up Patterns consist of:

1 1 ½ 1

2 WHOLE STEPS + 1 HALF STEP + 1 WHOLE STEP

Tonic Key: A major tune-up pattern may begin from any key on the keyboard. This beginning, or TONIC key, names the tune-up with its letter name.

All twelve of the major tune-ups appear below and on page 57. Practice *TUNE-UP EXERCISE NO. 2* in each of these positions during the next several weeks.

TUNE-UP EXERCISE NO. 2

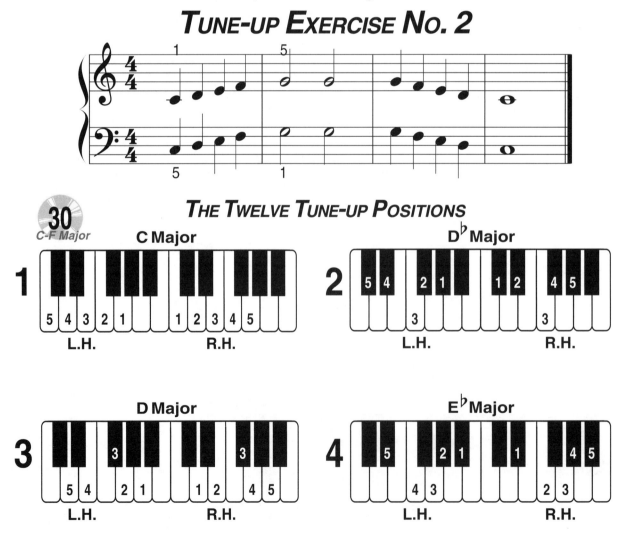

THE TWELVE TUNE-UP POSITIONS

30 *C-F Major*

1 C Major
5 4 3 2 1   1 2 3 4 5
L.H.   R.H.

2 D♭ Major
5 4 2 1 1 2 4 5
3   3
L.H.   R.H.

3 D Major
3   3
5 4 2 1 1 2 4 5
L.H.   R.H.

4 E♭ Major
5 2 1 1 4 5
4 3   2 3
L.H.   R.H.

E Major

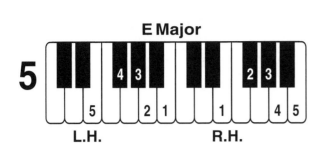

5 L.H. R.H.

F Major

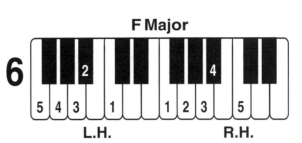

6 L.H. R.H.

31
G♭-C Major

G♭ Major

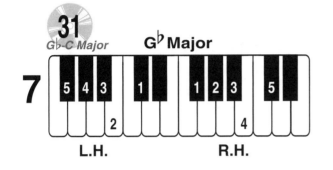

7 L.H. R.H.

G Major

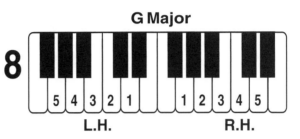

8 L.H. R.H.

A♭ Major

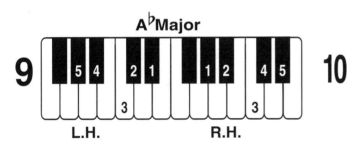

9 L.H. R.H.

A Major

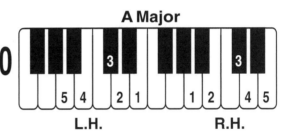

10 L.H. R.H.

B♭ Major

11 L.H. R.H.

B Major

12 L.H. R.H.

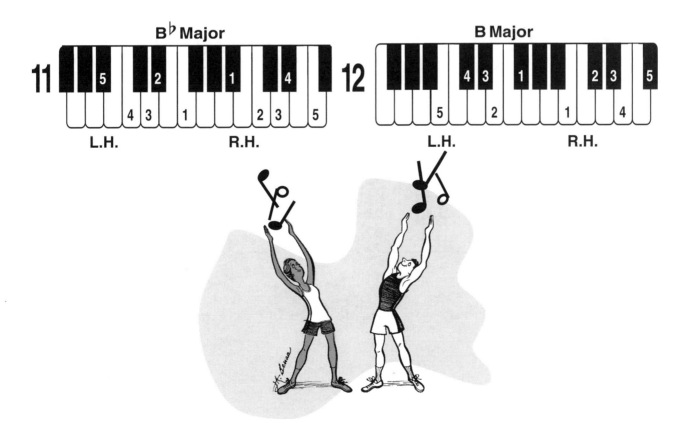

57

Writing Practice

 Write **X**'s on each key needed to complete the following major tune-up patterns. Remember, each tune-up contains: **2 whole steps + 1 half step + 1 whole step.**

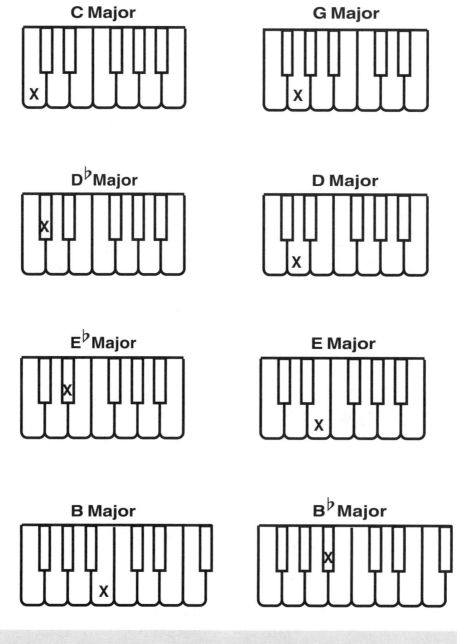

C Major

G Major

D♭ Major

D Major

E♭ Major

E Major

B Major

B♭ Major

Check pages 56 - 57 to be sure that you have written each tune-up correctly. Then, play and listen to each of these tune-ups.

2364

Improvising on Tune-up Patterns

☀ More New Melodies ☀

You can create new melodies by playing DIFFERENT TONES along with the rhythm of any familiar melody.

1 CLAP this rhythm from
LIGHTLY ROW as you say "quarter," etc.

32 Audio Trk Repeats *LIGHTLY ROW*

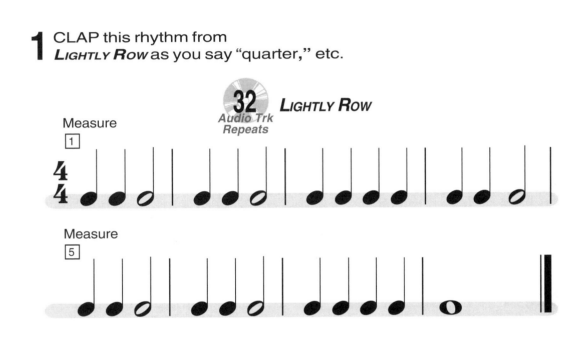

Measure [1]

Measure [5]

2 POSITION your hands on any of
the major tune-ups shown on pages 56 - 57.

3 Play any keys of your tune-up in time to the rhythm
of *LIGHTLY ROW.* Improvise several melodies in one
hand and then in the other hand. End in measure 8
on your tune-up's TONIC (lowest key) to make your
melody sound "complete."

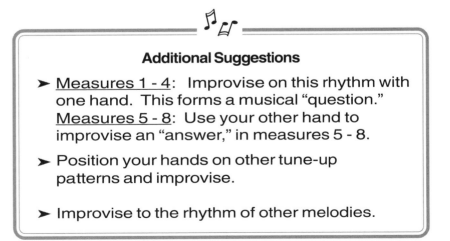

Additional Suggestions

➤ Measures 1 - 4: Improvise on this rhythm with
one hand. This forms a musical "question."
Measures 5 - 8: Use your other hand to
improvise an "answer," in measures 5 - 8.

➤ Position your hands on other tune-up
patterns and improvise.

➤ Improvise to the rhythm of other melodies.

59

Playing A Duet

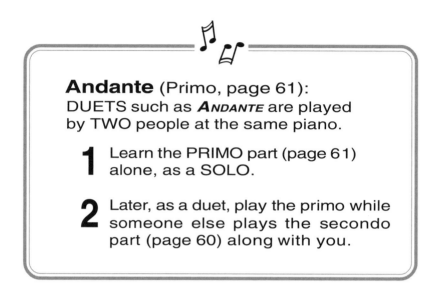

Andante (Primo, page 61):
DUETS such as ***ANDANTE*** are played
by TWO people at the same piano.

1 Learn the PRIMO part (page 61) alone, as a SOLO.

2 Later, as a duet, play the primo while someone else plays the secondo part (page 60) along with you.

ANDANTE
(Secondo—Second Player's Part)

Anton Diabelli

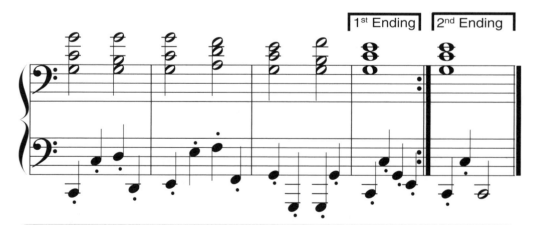

Andante:

"At a walking pace" or "moderately slow." This word refers to the TEMPO, or speed, at which this piece should be played after you have learned it.

Octave

A pair of keys eight letter names apart forms an OCTAVE. Both keys have the same letter name.

8va---

8va above a note means play that note one octave HIGHER than written.

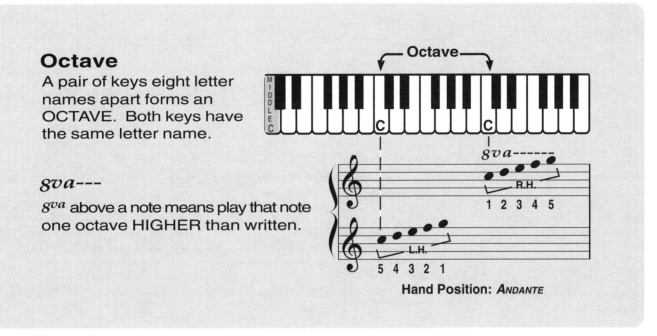

Hand Position: *ANDANTE*

In *ANDANTE,* your left and right hands both play in the treble clef. Play your right hand one octave higher than written, as the marking "*8va*" indicates.

ANDANTE
(Primo—Play on Upper Keyboard)

Anton Diabelli

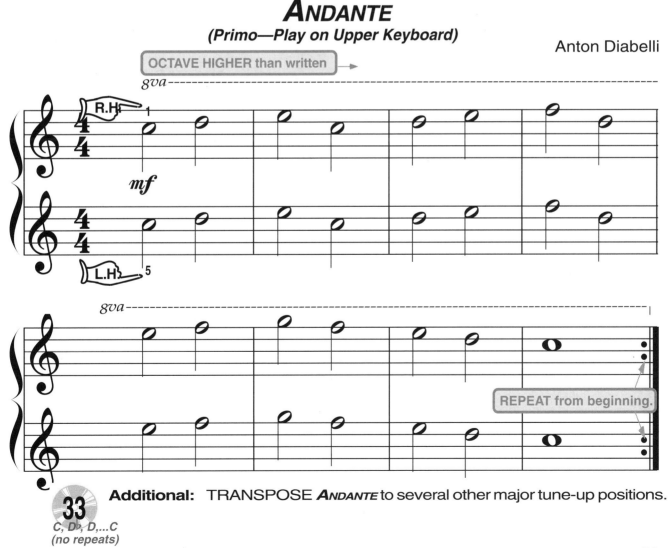

33

C, D♭, D,...C
(no repeats)

Additional: TRANSPOSE *ANDANTE* to several other major tune-up positions.

2364

Repetitions and Sequences

REPETITION: A pattern that repeats exactly.

1 *FRERE JACQUES* begins with a PATTERN and REPETITION (shown below). Play and listen to this example:

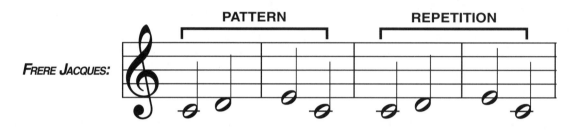

(For this discussion, *FRERE JACQUES* is now written in half notes instead of the quarter notes of page 39.)

SEQUENCE: A pattern that repeats on different keys.

2 *ANDANTE* begins with the same pattern as *FRERE JACQUES*. However, *ANDANTE* follows this pattern with a SEQUENCE instead of an exact repetition. Play and listen to this example:

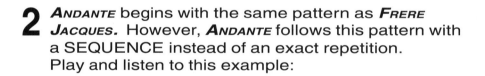

Find other examples of patterns and sequences in *LIGHTLY ROW, HEY LOLLY,* and *NIGHT COMES BACK, AGAIN.*

2364

Composing With Sequences

Use notes from this tune-up:

C Major Tune-up

1 Notice the two STEPS and one SKIP in the pattern below.

2 Below, begin on F and write a sequence for the preceding pattern.

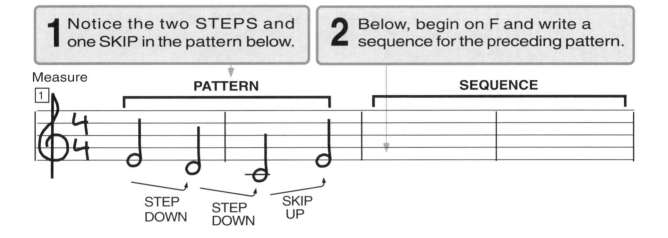

Measure
1

PATTERN

SEQUENCE

STEP DOWN   STEP DOWN   SKIP UP

Measure
5

2 HALF NOTES PER MEASURE

End on C (tonic).

3 Complete this composition by adding two half notes in each of measures 5 - 7.

Play measures 1 - 8, above, to hear the new melody you have just written.

4 Compose, then play, another pattern-and-sequence melody.

Use notes from this tune-up:

F Major Tune-up

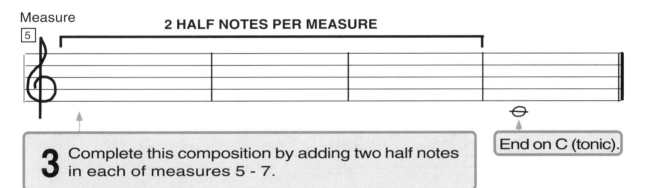

PATTERN   SEQUENCE   CONTINUE MELODY

1

FINISH MELODY: a) begin measures 5 - 6 the same as measures 1 - 2 ("parallel answer"), or, instead,
b) begin measures 5 - 6 differently than measures 1 - 2 ("contrasting answer").

5

63

Key Signatures

Flat all B's & E's.

A group of flats or sharps that follow a clef sign are called a KEY SIGNATURE. Key signatures indicate which keys to flat or sharp throughout a composition. Key signatures can also tell the NAME of the tune-up, or the "KEY," in which a composition is written.
(See "Identifying Major Tune-ups," below and on page 66).

Sharp all F's & C's.

♭ **Flat Key Signatures:**

There are seven different flat key signatures. Each signature is written in a LEFT-TO-RIGHT pattern that begins from B♭, as shown below.

Identifying Major Tune-ups:

Name the signature's NEXT-TO-LAST flat to identify the major tune-up the signature represents.

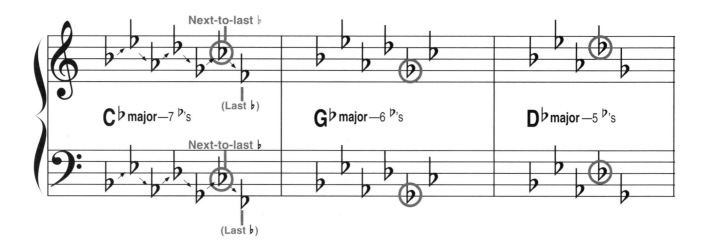

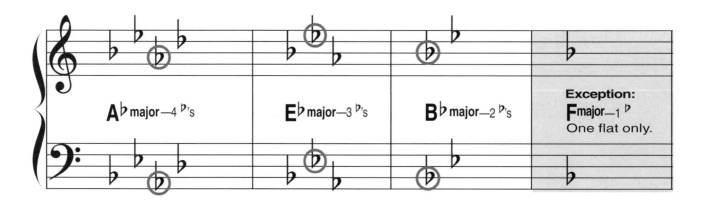

Before playing **MY DOG,** play the tune-up indicated by the key signature. Then, practice **MY DOG** hands alone and hands together.

F Major Tune-up

34 MY DOG

American Folk Song

mp (MEZZO PIANO: Medium soft)

mf   *f*

CRESCENDO: Get louder gradually.

Additional: Vary the DYNAMICS (choosing from *f, mf, mp, p,* etc.) as you play this piece.

Transpose **MY DOG** to several other tune-up positions.

65

Sharps

Sharp Key Signatures:
There are seven different sharp key signatures. Each signature is written in a LEFT-TO-RIGHT pattern that begins from F#, as shown below.

Identifying Major Tune-ups:
Name the line or space directly ABOVE a key signature's FINAL SHARP to identify the major tune-up the signature represents.

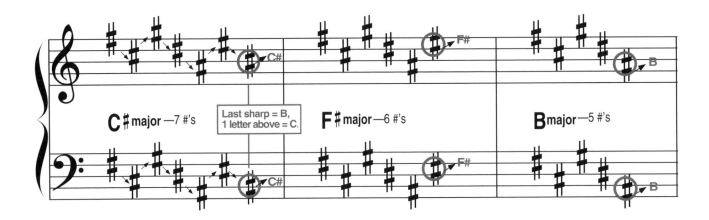

C# major —7 #'s

Last sharp = B, 1 letter above = C.

F# major —6 #'s

B major —5 #'s

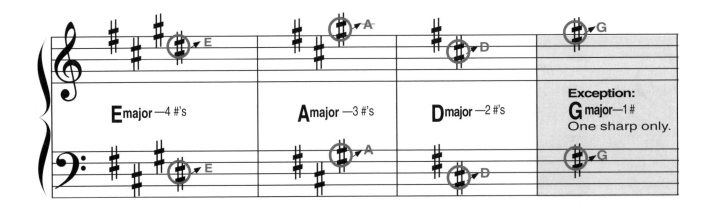

E major —4 #'s

A major —3 #'s

D major —2 #'s

Exception:
G major —1 #
One sharp only.

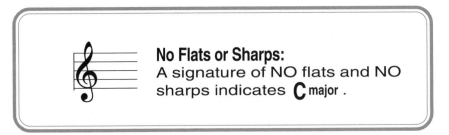

No Flats or Sharps:
A signature of NO flats and NO sharps indicates **C** major.

Slurs

Slur:
A SLUR is a curved line above or below TWO or more DIFFERENT NOTES. Slurred notes are played in a smooth, connected, LEGATO manner.

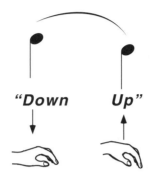

"Down   *Up"*

In two-note slurs, the first note is usually emphasized and the second note is then played a little more softly. Drop your wrist slightly as you play the first note and lift your wrist as you play the softer second note.

When first practicing *The Cuckoo,* say "down" as you lower your wrist and "up" as you raise your wrist.

35 *The Cuckoo*

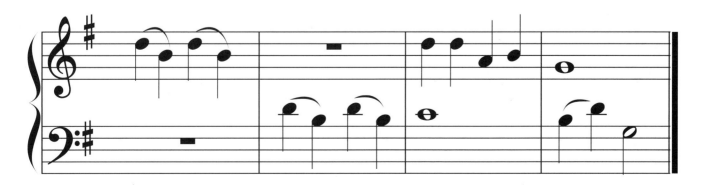

2364

Tied Notes

Tie:

A tie is a curved line between two or more consecutive notes on the SAME LINE or SPACE. Ties COMBINE the RHYTHMIC VALUES of notes.

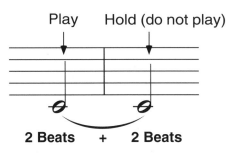

Play   Hold (do not play)

2 Beats   +   2 Beats

Play and HOLD the first note in a tied group for the total value of all the notes.

D MAJOR

36 HUNGARIAN FOLK SONG

Folk Song

SLUR: 2 notes occupy DIFFERENT lines/spaces. Play BOTH notes.

TIE: Play first note only and HOLD.

Repeat *p*

68

Writing Your Own Melody

☼ Composing a Melody ☼ ---

You can compose new melodies by writing DIFFERENT TONES for the RHYTHM of any familiar melody.

To write a melody using the rhythmic pattern of *HUNGARIAN FOLK SONG:*

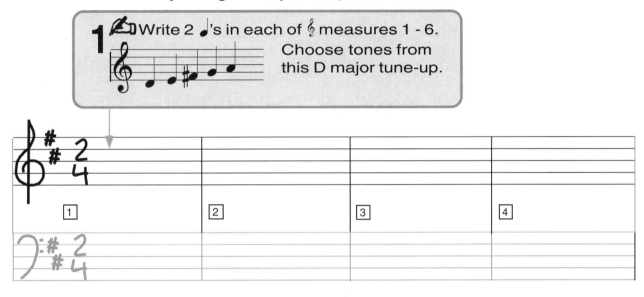

1 🎹 Write 2 ♩'s in each of ⁶⁄₈ measures 1 - 6. Choose tones from this D major tune-up.

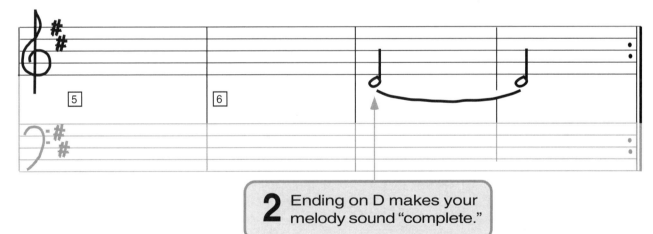

2 Ending on D makes your melody sound "complete."

♪♫ ---

Composition Hints

➤ As you're composing, play and listen to your melody frequently.

➤ Try changing some of your notes to other notes. If you prefer these new notes, write them in place of the original notes. Use a pencil so you can make changes easily.

Additional: Write a left hand part to go with your melody, as in *HUNGARIAN FOLK SONG* (page 68).

2364

Dotted Half Notes

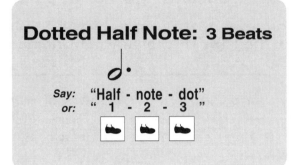

Dotted Half Note: 3 Beats

Say: "Half - note - dot"
or: " 1 - 2 - 3 "

37 *ANDANTINO, OP. 100, NO. 19*
(Adapted)

Burgmuller

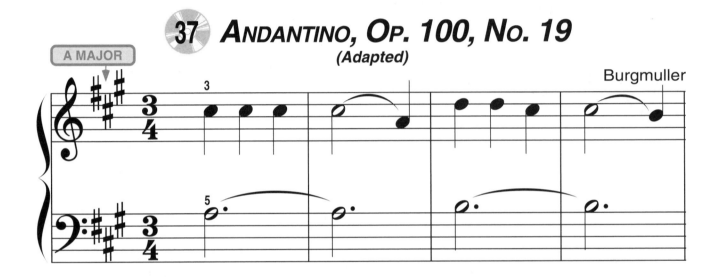

Additional: Improvise new melodies. Play several of these new melodies, right hand alone. Then, play the original bass clef part with your left hand, as you improvise more new melodies with your right hand.

Transpose *ANDANTINO* down one half step to A♭ major.

Practice *WALTZ* hands alone, then hands together.

Quarter Rest: ❳ = ♩

Silence for 1 beat in $\frac{2}{4}$, $\frac{3}{4}$, or $\frac{4}{4}$ time.

UPBEAT MEASURE:
A beginning measure with FEWER BEATS than the time signature designates. First beat, or DOWNBEAT, is "missing."

38 WALTZ

German Folk Song

QUARTER REST
Say: "quarter."

L.H. (ms. 4-8) imitates R.H. (ms. 1-4).

L.H. (ms. 12-14) imitates R.H. (ms. 8-10).

The number of beats missing from an UPBEAT measure usually appear in the FINAL measure.

71

Review
(Pages 35 - 71)

1. Write a WHOLE NOTE in the bass and treble clefs for each letter. Play these notes in their proper registers.

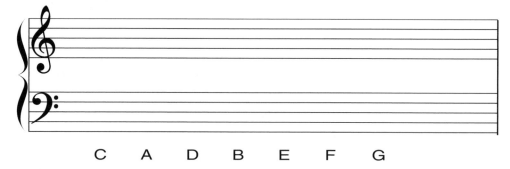

C   A   D   B   E   F   G

2. Label each curved line SLUR or TIE:

_____   _____   _____   _____

3. Write in the BARLINES for this rhythmic pattern so that four beats occur in each measure.

4. Write the pattern of seven FLATS in the blank measure.

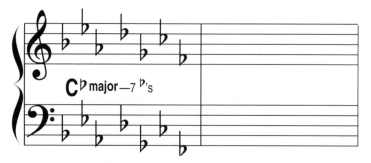

2364

5. To identify a flat key signature, name the _____ flat.

6. Write the pattern of seven SHARPS in the blank measure.

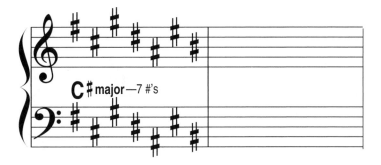

C♯ major—7 #'s

7. To identify a sharp key signature, count one letter-name above the _____ sharp.

8. A melodic pattern that repeats on different keys is called a _____.

9. Two neighboring keys with no other key between form a _____.

10. Two keys eight letter names apart are called an _____.

Major Scales

A **TETRACHORD** consists of: 2 WHOLE STEPS + 1 HALF STEP.
Two **TETRACHORDS** that lie a whole step apart form a **MAJOR SCALE.**

1 Play this C major scale with fingers 2 - 5 of your left and right hands (no thumbs), as shown.

2 Play and memorize the major scales on pages 74 and 76 during the next few weeks.

Playing Sharp Scales:

➤ Your left hand begins each new scale by repeating the preceding scale's upper tetrachord.

➤ Your right hand ADDS one NEW SHARP in each scale with finger 4.

➤ C major is the only major scale with no black keys.

39 *SHARP-KEY SCALES*

2364

Writing Sharp Key Signatures

Each sharp-key scale has a corresponding key signature that tells which tones are sharped. This key signature is named by the LINE or SPACE just ABOVE its final sharp (review page 66).

Key Signature Names: Only C-sharp major and F-sharp major include the word "sharp" in their names. All other major keys do not include the word "sharp" in their names. These are C major, G major, D major, A major, E major, and B major.

>  In the blank measures below, copy and identify each sharp key signature.

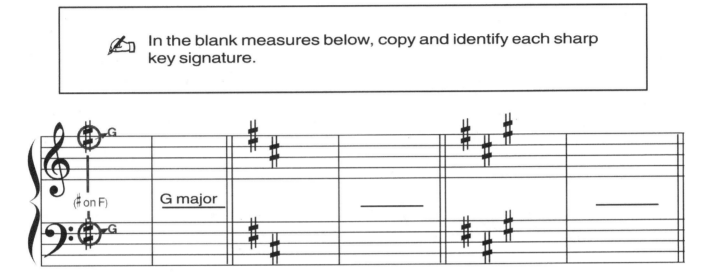

(♯ on F)   G major

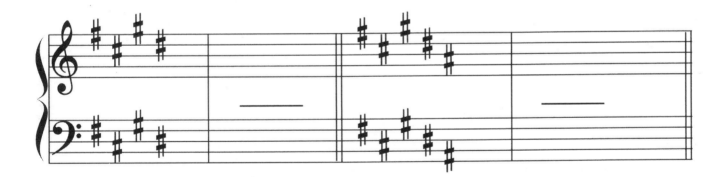

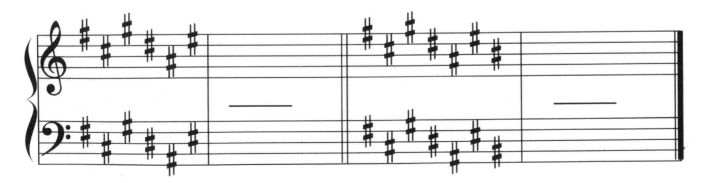

2364

40 FLAT-KEY SCALES

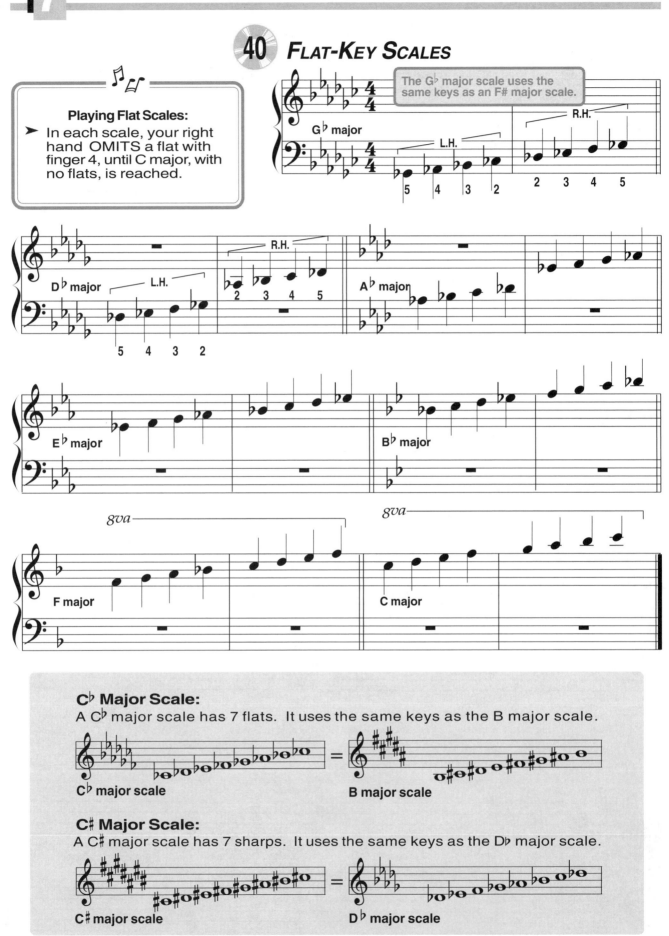

Playing Flat Scales:
➤ In each scale, your right hand OMITS a flat with finger 4, until C major, with no flats, is reached.

The G♭ major scale uses the same keys as an F# major scale.

C♭ Major Scale:
A C♭ major scale has 7 flats. It uses the same keys as the B major scale.

C♭ major scale = B major scale

C♯ Major Scale:
A C♯ major scale has 7 sharps. It uses the same keys as the D♭ major scale.

C♯ major scale = D♭ major scale

Writing Flat Key Signatures

Each flat-key scale has a corresponding key signature that tells which tones are flatted. Flat key signatures are named by their NEXT-TO-LAST FLAT (review page 64). An exception is the key of F major with only the one flat, B♭, in its signature.

Key Signature Names: All flat key signatures except F major contain the word "flat" in their names. These are C-flat major, G-flat major, D-flat major, A-flat major, E-flat major, and B-flat major.

> 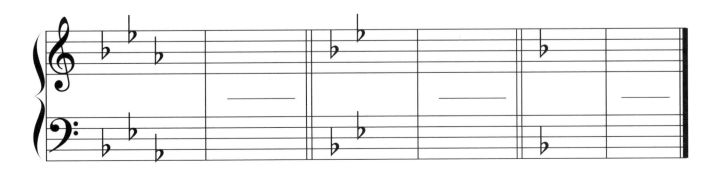 In the blank measures below, copy and identify each flat key signature.

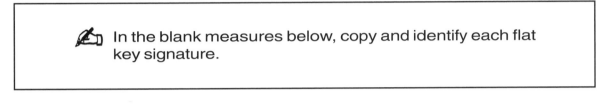

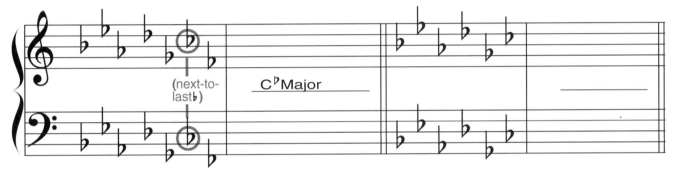

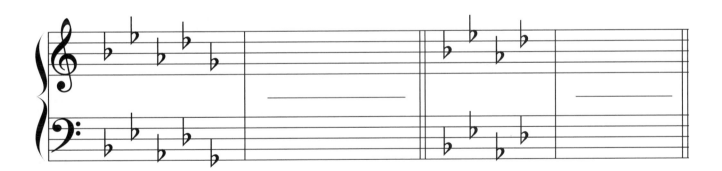

2364

Phrases

Phrase:
A PHRASE is a group of notes that form a MUSICAL UNIT similar to a word phrase. Phrases are often indicated with extended slur lines.

VIVE L'AMOUR uses tones of a B♭ major scale. This song is therefore in the KEY OF B♭ MAJOR. Notice that the melody of *VIVE L'AMOUR* extends beyond one octave (to tone C) in measures 6 and 14. As you practice this song, listen to the way the notes in each phrase "fit together" as a musical unit. Follow the indicated fingering.

B♭ MAJOR:
Flat all B's and E's.

41 VIVE L'AMOUR

French Folk Song

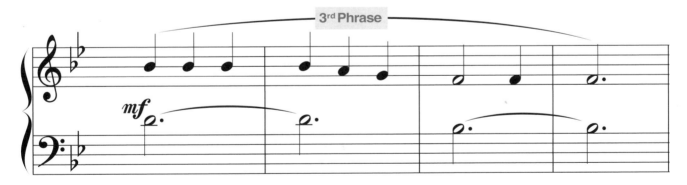

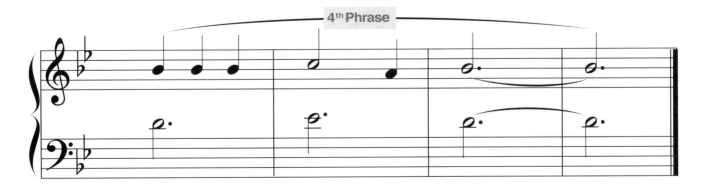

79

Eighth Notes

An EIGHTH NOTE (♪) has HALF the value of a QUARTER
NOTE. TWO EIGHTH notes equal ONE QUARTER note.
Eighth notes may appear separately (♪) or together (♫).

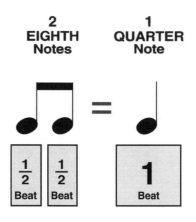

| 2
EIGHTH
Notes | 1
QUARTER
Note |

Say: *"Quar - ter   eighth eighth two - eighths"*

or: *"1   &   2   &   3   &"*

I Am The Very Model (page 81):

1 Say "eighth two-eighths" etc., as you clap
a few measures of *I AM THE VERY MODEL*
(page 81).

2 Your right hand plays the upward-stemmed
treble clef notes and your left hand plays
the downward-stemmed bass clef notes.
POSITION YOUR HANDS over the treble
and bass notes ACCORDING TO THE
FINGERING indicated in the music. You will
notice that *I AM THE VERY MODEL* uses all
seven notes of the G major scale.

42 I Am The Very Model
(Adapted from Pirates of Penzance)

Gilbert and Sullivan

G MAJOR: Sharp all F's.

Eighth Rest

I am the ver - y mod-el of a mod-ern Ma - jor Gen-e - ral, I've

in - for - ma - tion, veg - e - ta - ble, an - i - mal and min - e - ral; I

know the kings of Eng - land and I quote the fights his - tor - i - cal from

ACCIDENTAL: Added sharp or flat not found in key signature.

Mar - a thon to Wa - ter - loo, in or - der cat - e - go - ri - cal.

NATURAL SIGN (♮): CANCELS previous sharp or flat.

Minor Scales

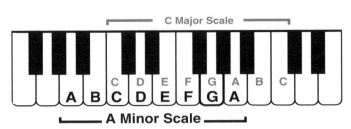

C Major Scale

A Minor Scale

For every major scale, there is a NATURAL MINOR scale that shares the same keys, but begins and ends a SKIP lower. For example, the A minor scale uses the same tones as a C major scale, but begins and ends on A instead of C. Play and listen to the C major and A minor scales written below.

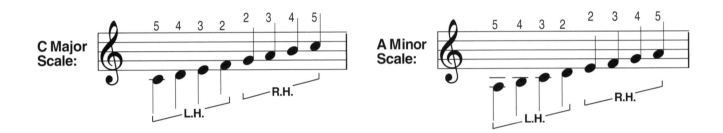

C Major Scale: 5 4 3 2   2 3 4 5   L.H.   R.H.

A Minor Scale: 5 4 3 2   2 3 4 5   L.H.   R.H.

Minor Key Signatures:

A major and minor scale that share the same keys also share the same key signatures. These are called RELATIVE MAJOR and RELATIVE MINOR scales.

Identifying Minor Scales: ONE SKIP (or three half steps) BELOW the major signature's name is the relative minor signature's name.

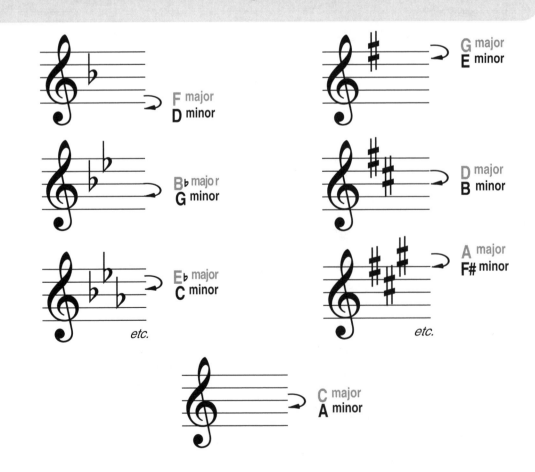

F major / D minor

Bb major / G minor

Eb major / C minor   etc.

G major / E minor

D major / B minor

A major / F# minor   etc.

C major / A minor

Though a major and minor scale may share the same keys, each can create very different effects: Minor often sounds sad or sombre, while major frequently seems cheerful and happy. Listen to the sound of minor as you practice **SPANISH TUNE.** Notice the contrast when measure 5 momentarily introduces a major sound. As you play, observe the dynamic markings. Notice the time signature shift to $\frac{4}{4}$ and then back to $\frac{3}{4}$ on the second line of this song.

1ˢᵗ Ending & 2ⁿᵈ Ending:

At repeat sign in 1ˢᵗ ending, return to 𝄆 at beginning of piece. REPEAT from here but substitute 2ⁿᵈ ending for 1ˢᵗ ending.

43 SPANISH TUNE
(D Minor)

Folk

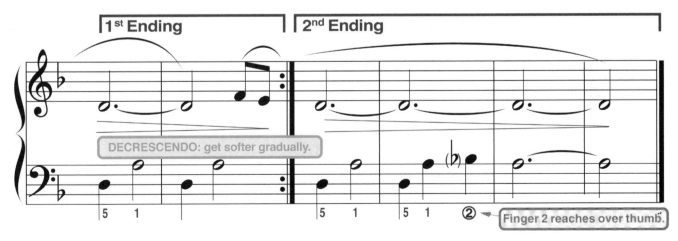

Practice **ERIE CANAL** hands alone then hands together. Notice that your left hand begins on low E, the second E to the left of middle C.

44 ERIE CANAL

American

Key of E minor.
Sharp all F's.

I've got a mule, her name is Sal, Fif - teen miles on the E - rie Ca - nal. She's a good old work - er and a good old pal, Fif - teen miles on the E - rie Ca - nal.

2364

Intervals

Any two tones TOGETHER form an INTERVAL.

HARMONIC INTERVAL:

Two tones played at the **same time.**

MELODIC INTERVAL:

Two tones played **consecutively.**

Naming Intervals

Intervals can be named by counting the number of letter names from the lower key up to and including the higher key.

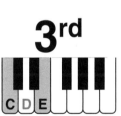

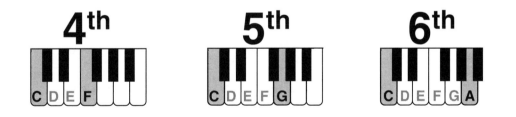

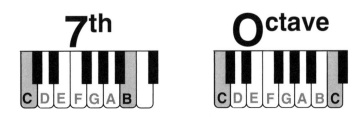

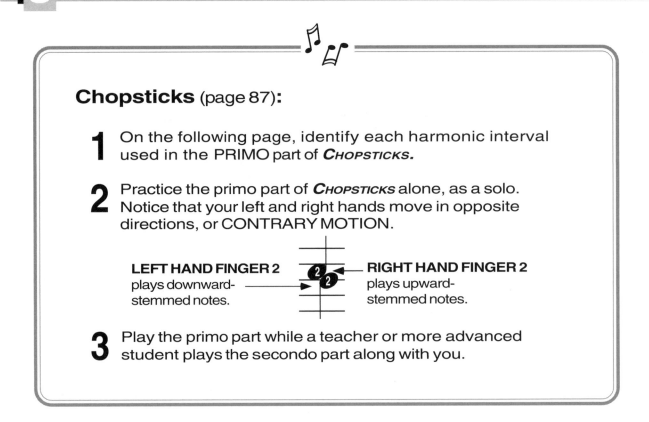

Chopsticks (page 87):

1 On the following page, identify each harmonic interval used in the PRIMO part of *CHOPSTICKS.*

2 Practice the primo part of *CHOPSTICKS* alone, as a solo. Notice that your left and right hands move in opposite directions, or CONTRARY MOTION.

LEFT HAND FINGER 2 plays downward-stemmed notes.

RIGHT HAND FINGER 2 plays upward-stemmed notes.

3 Play the primo part while a teacher or more advanced student plays the secondo part along with you.

(Secondo—Second Player's Part)

2364

CHOP STICKS
(Primo—Student's Part)

Seconds and Thirds

Second:
Notes on an ADJACENT LINE and SPACE form a SECOND.

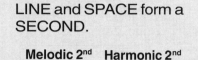

Melodic 2nd Harmonic 2nd

(Both notes play simultaneously.)

(A "MINOR 2nd" spans a half STEP. A "MAJOR 2nd" spans a whole STEP.)

Third:
Notes on SUCCESSIVE LINES or SPACES form a THIRD.

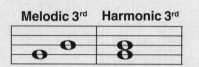

Melodic 3rd Harmonic 3rd

(A "MINOR 3rd" spans one-and-a half STEPS. A "MAJOR 3rd" spans two whole STEPS.)

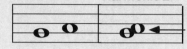 Write "2nd" or "3rd" for each interval below.

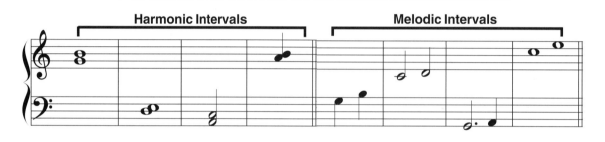

Harmonic Intervals   Melodic Intervals

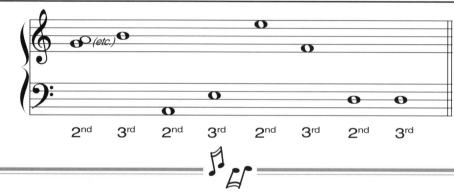 Form HARMONIC intervals by adding a note directly above each of these notes. (**Exception:** In harmonic 2nds, upper note appears to the right of lower note.)

2nd   3rd   2nd   3rd   2nd   3rd   2nd   3rd

J'ai Du Bon Tabac & Celebration Song (page 89):

Identify the 2nds and 3rds in the accompaniment of *J'AI DU BON TABAC* and *CELEBRATION SONG,* then practice each song. Tune up in A♭ major before playing *J'AI DU BON TABAC.* Notice how this melody begins with the same pattern as *FRERE JACQUES* and *ANDANTE.*

As you practice *CELEBRATION SONG,* notice how your right hand plays outside the G major tune-up position—finger numbers in the music will guide you.

46 J'AI DU BON TABAC

French Folk Song

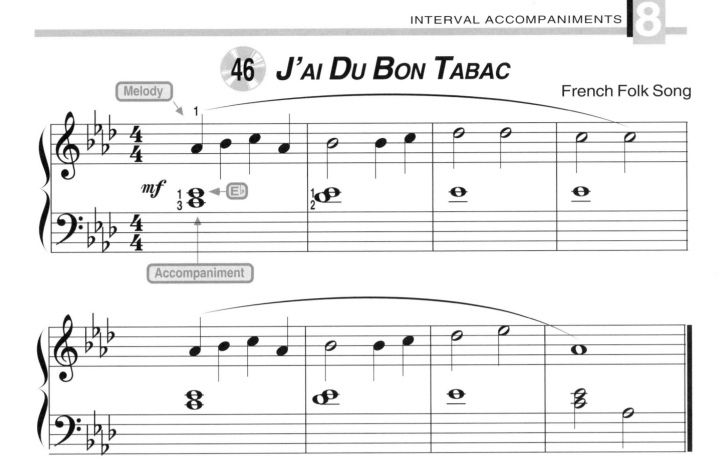

Melody

Accompaniment

47 CELEBRATION SONG

Folk Tune

R.H. 1 on D

FERMATA: Hold note longer than its regular value.

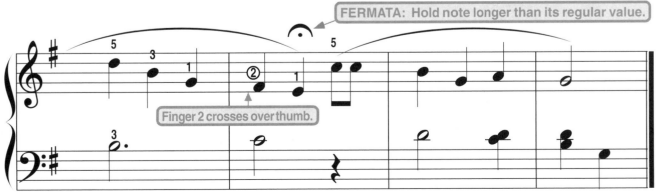

Finger 2 crosses over thumb.

2364

Fourths and Fifths

Fourth:
A LINE and SPACE SEPARATED by another line and space form a FOURTH.

Melodic 4th   Harmonic 4th

(A "PERFECT 4th" spans two-and-a-half STEPS.)

Fifth:
Two LINES with another line BETWEEN or two SPACES with another space BETWEEN form a FIFTH.

Melodic 5th   Harmonic 5th

(A "PERFECT 5th" spans three-and-a-half STEPS.)

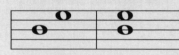 Below, write "4th" or "5th" for each interval.

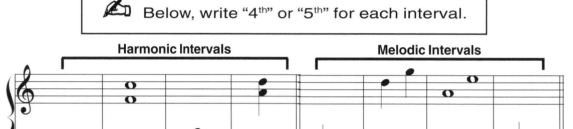

Harmonic Intervals   Melodic Intervals

___   ___   ___   ___   ___   ___   ___   ___

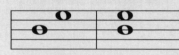 Form HARMONIC intervals by adding a note above each of these notes.

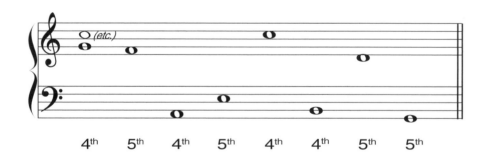

4th   5th   4th   5th   4th   4th   5th   5th

Music Box (page 91):

The accompaniment in *Music Box* uses both HARMONIC and MELODIC intervals. Identify these 2nds, 3rds, 4ths, and 5ths. Then, tune up in B♭ major and practice this piece hands alone and hands together. Notice that BOTH hands play in the TREBLE CLEF.

48 Music Box

Additional: Play *Music Box* in the highest register of the keyboard. Transpose *Music Box* to other keys.

Dotted Quarter Notes

A DOTTED QUARTER NOTE (𝅘𝅥.) gets ONE-AND-A-HALF beats in $\frac{2}{4}$, $\frac{3}{4}$, or $\frac{4}{4}$ time.

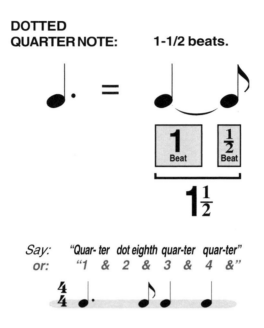

DOTTED QUARTER NOTE: 1-1/2 beats.

Hold the dotted quarters for their full value as you play **MICHAEL ROW THE BOAT ASHORE.**

49 MICHAEL ROW THE BOAT ASHORE

American Folk Song

Elvis Presley used this famous melody for his song *LOVE ME TENDER.* Notice that your right thumb begins outside the F major tune-up position on tone C instead of F. Your left hand also extends beyond the F major tune-up position in lines 3 and 4—the fingering in the music will guide you. Practice hands alone, then hands together.

50 AURA LEE

Folk Song

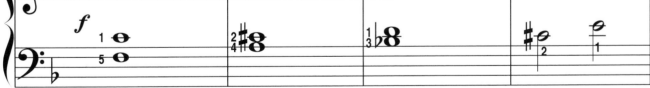

Ostinato Basses

1 Practice the LEFT HAND accompaniment from *JIG.*
Notice the alternating pairs of G and F fifths which form a repeating figure, or "OSTINATO".

Ostinato

2 Play the melody from *JIG,* right hand alone. Observe how the melody (along with the left hand accompaniment) shifts between white-key positions that begin from G and from F.

Five-Finger White-Key Positions

3 Play *JIG* as written.

51 *IRISH JIG*

94

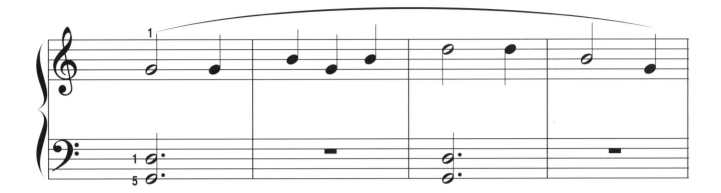

Repeat from beginning *p*

☀ **Improvising With An Ostinato** ☀

Play new melodies over the ostinato bass from *JIG.* Use
JIG's original rhythm in your melodies, then try your own
new rhythms.

Additional: Invert the positions of the melody and accompaniment—play the melody
with your left hand in the bass register and play the accompaniment with
your right hand in the treble register.

In *MELODY,* both hands play in the TREBLE CLEF. Practice *MELODY,* hands separately, then together. Work for a smooth, legato sound, observing the indicated dynamics and fingering.

> **TENUTO MARK (–):**
> Stress note, playing it a bit more firmly and holding for its full value.

52 *MELODY*

Dmitri Kabalevsky

C for COMMON TIME means ⁴⁄₄ time.

53 **Transpose:** Play in D major.

Improvising on Melody

1 Below, finish copying the accompaniment from *MELODY* (see page 96).

2 Use the tones of a C major tune-up to improvise NEW right hand MELODIES above the accompaniment. Follow the rhythm of *MELODY,* then try some new rhythms. WRITE a new melody in the treble clef.

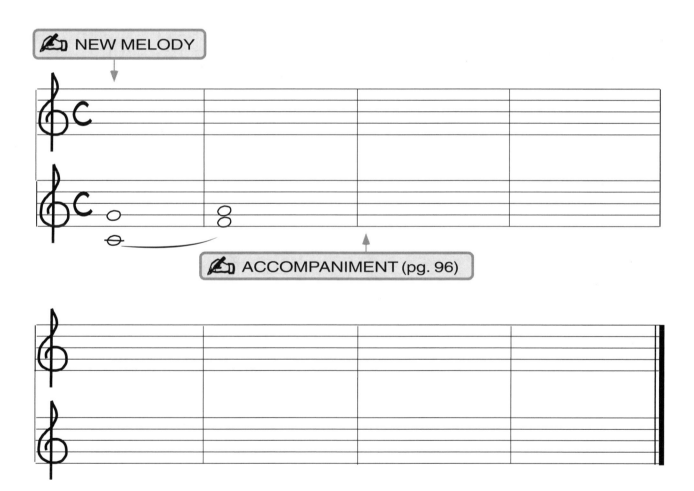

NEW MELODY

ACCOMPANIMENT (pg. 96)

1 The accompaniment in *Du, Du, Liegst Mir Im Herzen* is made up of intervals of a 5th and a 6th. To play the 6th, extend your little finger to the left, to F♯. Practice this left hand part alone several times.

Left Hand

2 Play your right hand alone then play *Du, Du, Liegst Mir Im Herzen* hands together.

54 *Du, Du, Liegst Mir Im Herzen*

German Folk Song

Count: "Half   Note   Dot..."

(R.H. holds as L.H. plays.)

...or: "Rest Quar-ter Quar-ter."

Sharp all F's.

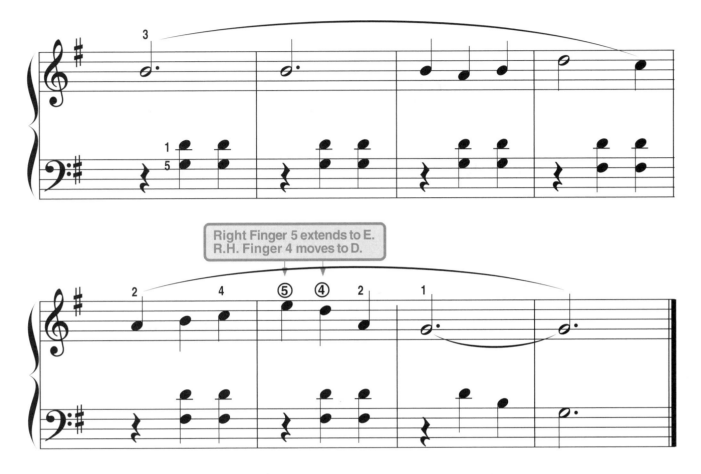

Right Finger 5 extends to E.
R.H. Finger 4 moves to D.

Transpose: Play in F major.

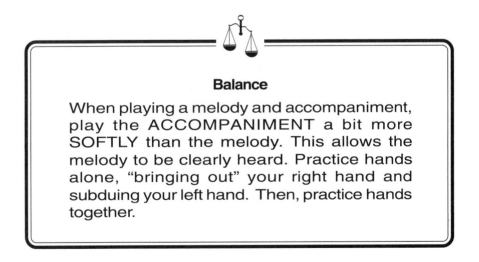

Balance

When playing a melody and accompaniment, play the ACCOMPANIMENT a bit more SOFTLY than the melody. This allows the melody to be clearly heard. Practice hands alone, "bringing out" your right hand and subduing your left hand. Then, practice hands together.

Playing Blues Melodies

1 In *CYAN BLUES*, your left hand plays 5^{ths} and 6^{ths} then holds, while your right hand plays. Notice how your left hand uses bass tones C (measures 1 - 4), F (measures 5 - 8), G (measures 9 -12), and, once again, C (measure 13 - 14). PRACTICE your left hand alone. Watch for left hand position shifts in measures 5, 9, and 13. Observe the STACCATO marks.

Left Hand

Bottom Bass Tones

 Staccato Mark:
A dot, or STACCATO mark, above or below a note means play the note in a short, DETACHED manner.
(If notes share a stem [♪], play both notes staccato).

2 The melody in *CYAN BLUES* uses tones C, D, and E from a C major scale. E, the third of these tones is flatted throughout most of the piece to create a BLUES sound. PRACTICE your right hand alone, observing the ACCENT marks, then play *CYAN BLUES,* hands together. (Your left hand begins in the lower bass clef, TWO octaves below your right hand).

Right Hand

Flatted 3rd ↑

> **Accent Mark:**
A wedge, or ACCENT, over or under a note means play the note sharply, with EMPHASIS.

55 Cyan Blues

With "Jazzy" Rhythmic Freedom

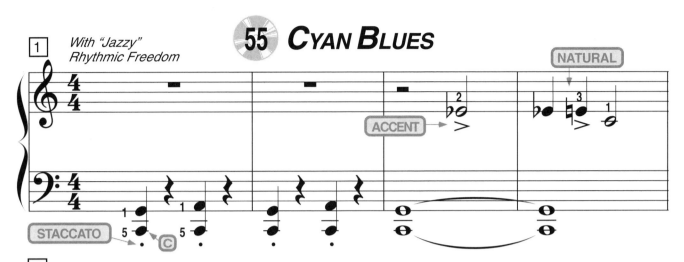

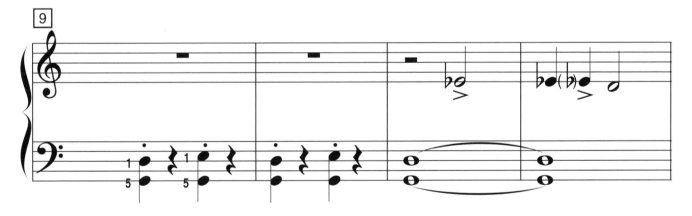

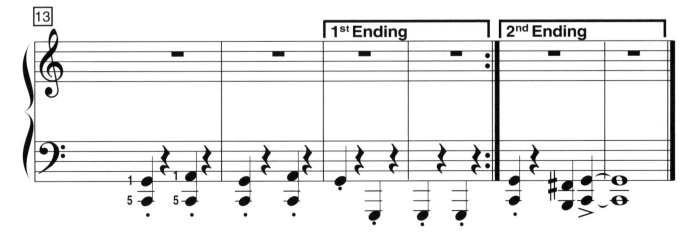

1st Ending   2nd Ending

101

Improvising the Blues

1 Play this BLUES TUNE-UP with your right hand. Notice that this new tune-up contains tones C, F, and G—the first, fourth, and fifth tones of a C major scale. It also contains the lowered third (E♭) and fifth (G♭) tones of a C major scale.

Blues Tune-Up

2 Play the BASS from *Cyan Blues*, as written below. In the measures where your left hand holds, improvise new melodies with your right hand. Use tones of the BLUES TUNE-UP.

56 *Cyan Blues—Bass*

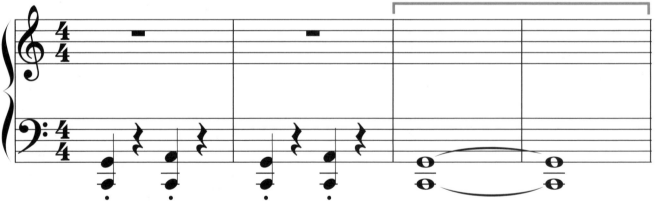

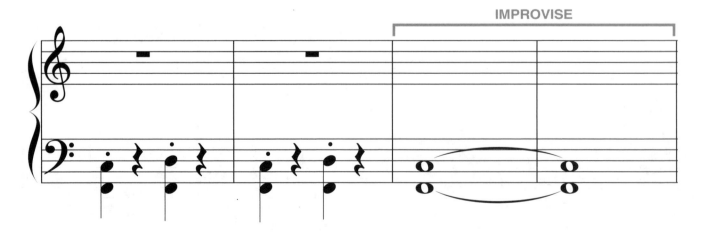

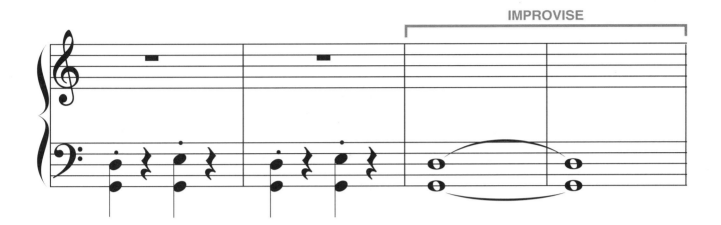

Major Chords

MAJOR CHORD:
The first, third, and fifth notes of a major scale form a MAJOR CHORD.

THE TWELVE MAJOR CHORDS

There are twelve major chords altogether. They may be grouped into FOUR different SETS according to their pattern of WHITE and BLACK keys:

Set 1: All White Keys

Set 2: Middle Key Black

Set 3: Middle White, Outside Black

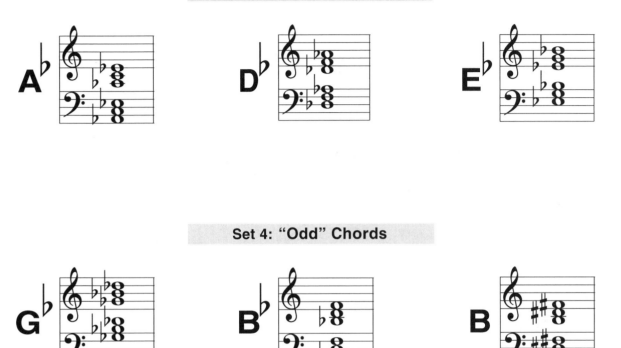

Set 4: "Odd" Chords

Broken and Block Chords

CHORD WALTZ contains BROKEN and BLOCK chords. During the next few weeks, play this piece in each major key. Begin with the chords of Set 1 (page 104) and continue through Sets 2 - 4.

Broken Chord   **Block Chord**

Left hand CROSSES OVER right hand to play this note.

CHORD WALTZ

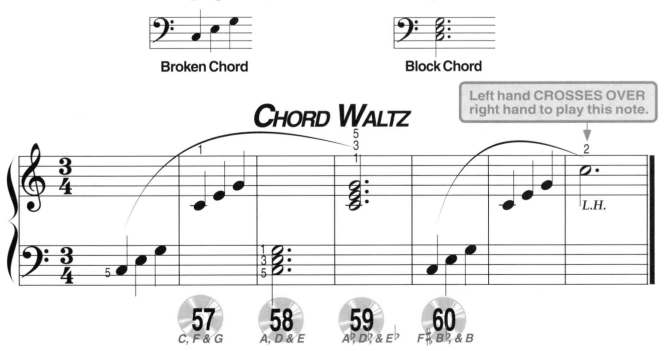

57   C, F & G

58   A, D & E

59   A♭, D♭ & E♭

60   F♯, B♭, & B

Chord Symbols: A LETTER over a melody note names the CHORD you should play with that note. An UPPER CASE letter that stands alone designates a MAJOR chord.

C ← Play a C major chord.

Practice the indicated chords with your LEFT hand then add the melody with your RIGHT hand in *Hot Cross Buns*, *Au Clair de la Lune,* and *Love Somebody.* Identify the indicated key signature before playing each song.

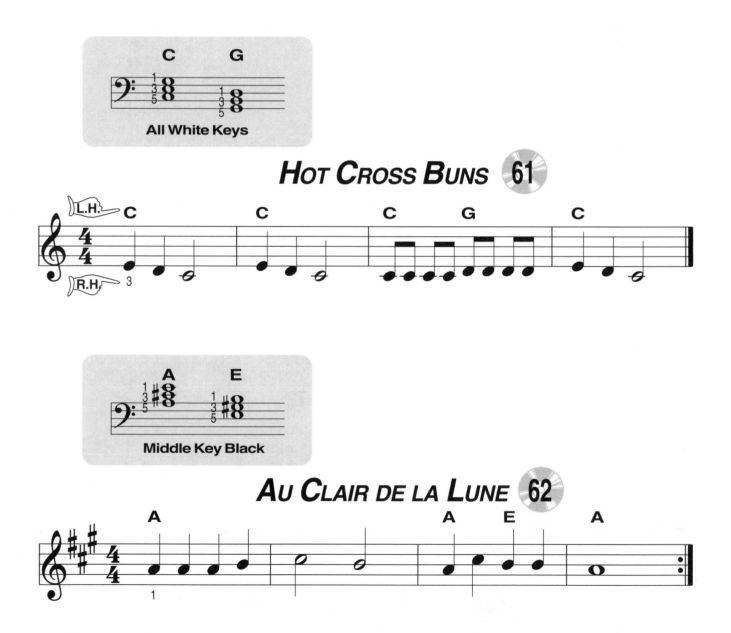

All White Keys

Hot Cross Buns 61

Middle Key Black

Au Clair de la Lune 62

2364

Middle White

LOVE SOMEBODY 63

"Odd Chords"

The B major and F♯ major chords that HARMONIZE *MY DOG* are notated in the bass clef. Play this piece hands alone, then hands together.

MY DOG 64

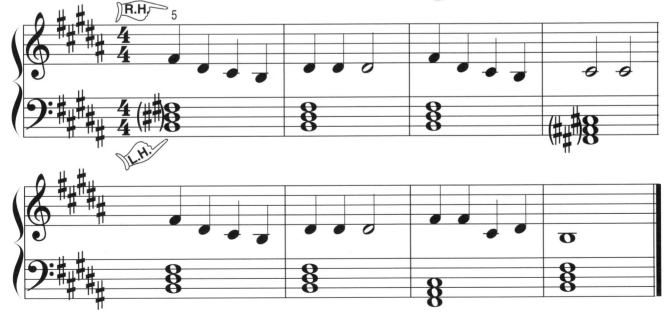

Balancing Melody and Chords

Remember to create a good BALANCE between melody and accompaniment by playing the chords a little more softly than the melody.

65 MARYANNE

Calypso Tune

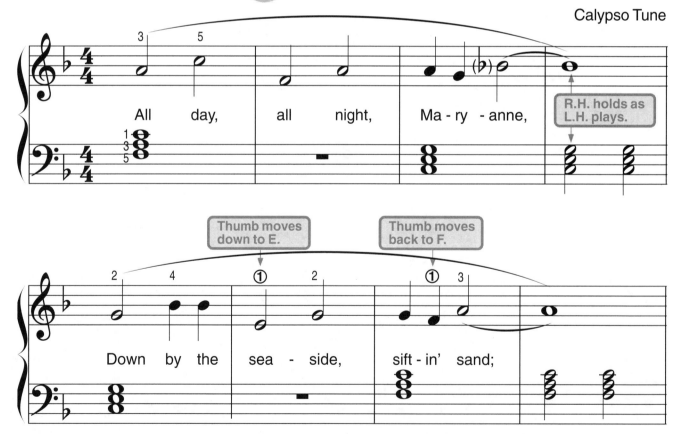

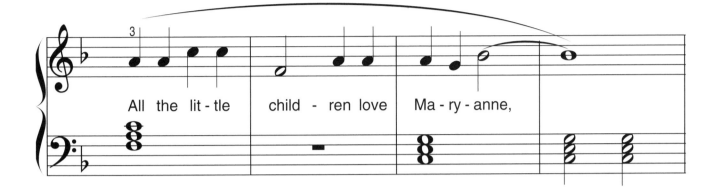

All the lit - tle   child - ren love   Ma - ry - anne,

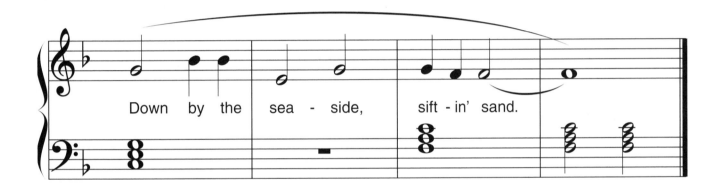

Down   by   the   sea - side,   sift - in' sand.

2364

YELLOW RIBBON

Folk Song

Round her neck she wore a yel-low rib-bon, She wore it in the

spring-time and in the month of May, And if you asked her

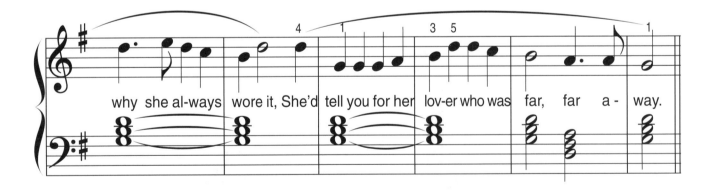

why she al-ways wore it, She'd tell you for her lov-er who was far, far a-way.

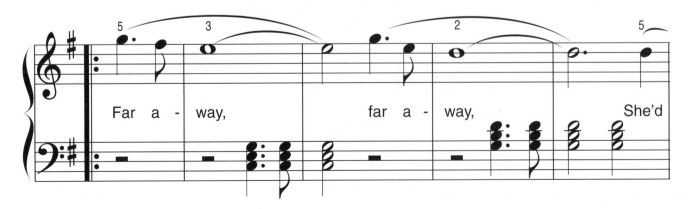

Far a - way, far a - way, She'd

110

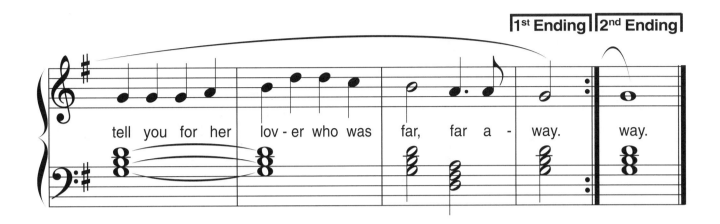

1st Ending | 2nd Ending

tell you for her | lov - er who was | far, far a - way. | way.

Chord Writing

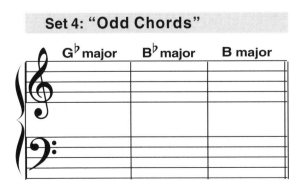

Write the indicated major chords in the treble and bass clefs (review pages 104 - 105),

Set 1: All White Keys

C major   F major   G major

Set 2: Middle Key Black

A major   D major   E major

Set 3: Middle White, Outside Black

A♭ major   D♭ major   E♭ major

Set 4: "Odd Chords"

G♭ major   B♭ major   B major

111

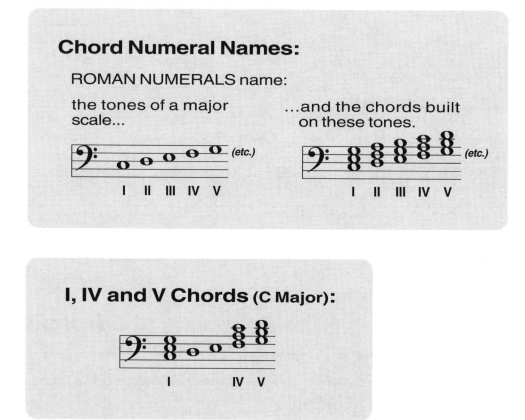

Chord Numeral Names:

ROMAN NUMERALS name:

the tones of a major scale...

...and the chords built on these tones.

I II III IV V

I II III IV V

I, IV and V Chords (C Major):

I   IV V

LITTLE BROWN JUG is accompanied with I, IV and V chords. Practice these chords in your left hand, then add the melody with your right hand.

67 LITTLE BROWN JUG

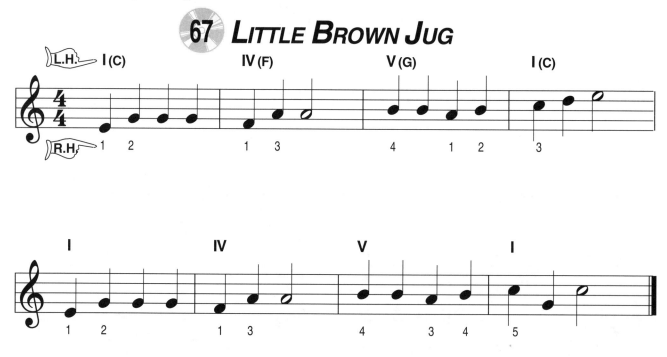

Chord Tone Melodies

Chord Tones:

The notes of a chord are called CHORD TONES.
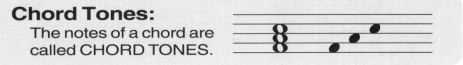

Melodies usually contain some or all of the chord tones from the harmonizing chord.

LOVE SOMEBODY:
The melody in this measure uses all three chord tones (C, E, and G).
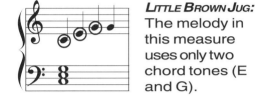

LITTLE BROWN JUG:
The melody in this measure uses only two chord tones (E and G).

1 Play the melodic variation of *LITTLE BROWN JUG* written below. Notice that each measure of this new melody is composed of tones from the accompanying chord.

2 Use chord tones from the accompanying chord to improvise your own new melodies with your right hand. Play this hand alone, then add the left hand accompaniment. Follow the original rhythm of *LITTLE BROWN JUG* in some of your melodies. In others, create your own rhythms.

68 LITTLE BROWN JUG
(Melodic Variation)

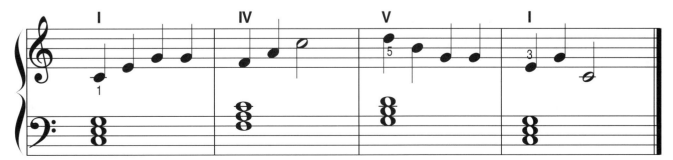

113

Chord Inversions

Chord Inversions:

Any chord may be INVERTED by changing the order of its tones.

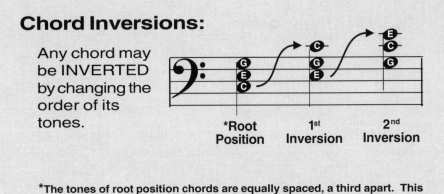

*Root Position   1st Inversion   2nd Inversion

*The tones of root position chords are equally spaced, a third apart. This equal spacing distinguishes ROOT position chords from their inverted forms.

Inverted IV Chords

A IV CHORD that follows a I chord is often inverted as shown. This makes it easier to move between I and IV chords, since both chords now share the same bottom note.

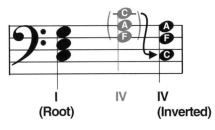

I (Root)   IV   IV (Inverted)

Create an inverted IV chord by moving a I chord's middle and top notes like this:

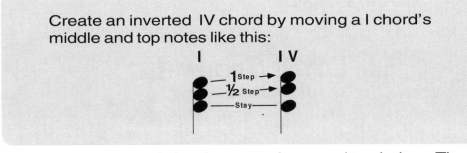

Learn to play the I-IV-I chord progression as written below. Then, transpose the I-IV-I chords to the remaining keys of E, F, F♯, G, A♭, A, B♭ and B major. *WHEN THE SAINTS GO MARCHING IN* (page 115) uses the IV and I chords.

69 I-IV-I CHORD PROGRESSION

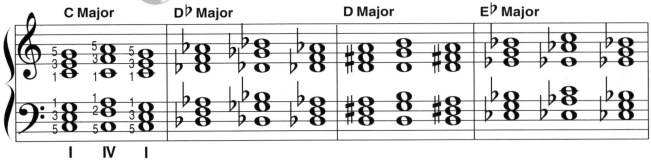

70 WHEN THE SAINTS GO MARCHING IN

Spiritual

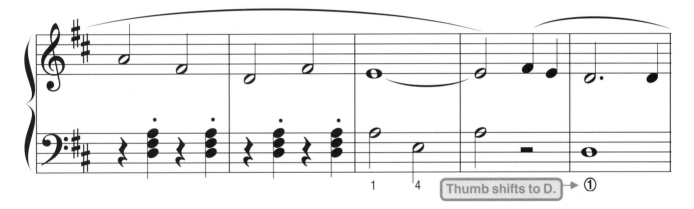

Thumb shifts to D. ➝ ①

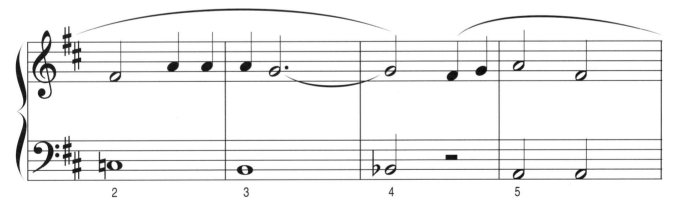

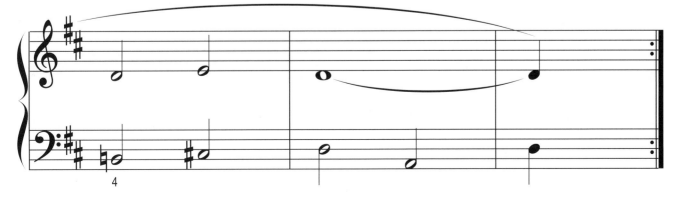

115

V⁷ Chords

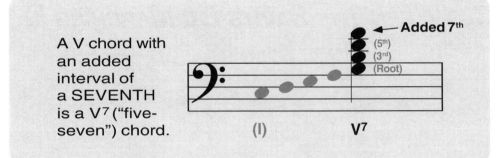

A V chord with an added interval of a SEVENTH is a V⁷ ("five-seven") chord.

Added 7th
(5th)
(3rd)
(Root)

(I)   V⁷

Inverted V⁷ Chords

V⁷ chords are often inverted. An inverted V⁷ usually omits one tone.

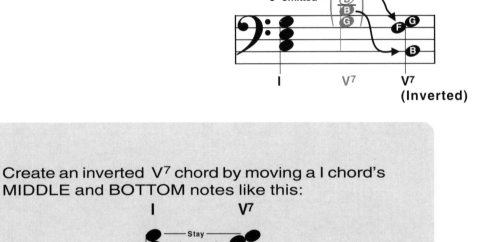

5th omitted

I   V⁷   V⁷
(Inverted)

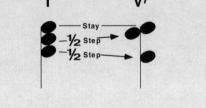

Create an inverted V⁷ chord by moving a I chord's MIDDLE and BOTTOM notes like this:

I   V⁷

Stay
½ Step
½ Step

Learn to play the I-V⁷-I chord progression as written below. Then, transpose the I-V⁷-I chords to the remaining keys of E, F, F♯, G, A♭, A, B♭ and B major.

71 *I-V⁷-I* CHORD PROGRESSION

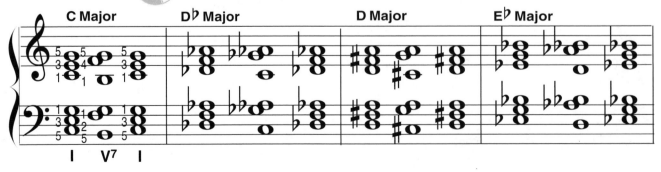

C Major   D♭ Major   D Major   E♭ Major

I   V⁷   I

Practice *FOLK SONG* with this V⁷ and I BLOCK CHORD BASS. Then, make up new melodies as you play this accompaniment.

72 *FOLK SONG*
(Block Chord Bass)

German

Change the BLOCK chord accompaniment of *FOLK SONG* to a WALTZ BASS, as shown below.

73 *FOLK SONG*
(Waltz Bass)

⁶⁄₈ *Time*

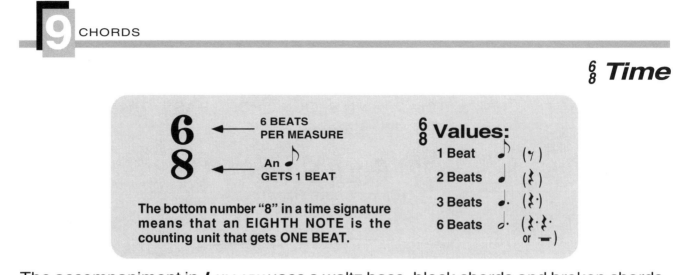

6 ← **6 BEATS PER MEASURE**

8 ← **An ♪ GETS 1 BEAT**

The bottom number "8" in a time signature means that an EIGHTH NOTE is the counting unit that gets ONE BEAT.

⁶⁄₈ Values:

1 Beat	♪	(𝄾)
2 Beats	♩	(𝄽)
3 Beats	♩.	(𝄽·)
6 Beats	𝅗𝅥.	(𝄽 𝄽· or ―)

The accompaniment in *LULLABY* uses a waltz bass, block chords and broken chords. Compare the broken chord at the end of line three with that in the song's next-to-last measure. As you practice, play the accompaniment a bit more softly than the melody.

Broken Chords I V⁷ or V⁷

74 *LULLABY*

French Folk Song

R.H. Fingering: 3

mp

Say: *"Quar - ter eighth*
or: *"4   5   6*
UPBEAT

quar - ter eighth three eighth notes"
1   2   3   4   5   6"

etc.

L.H. Fingering: 5   1   3

mf

mp

2364

As you practice **Row, Row, Row Your Boat,** notice how your left hand imitates part of the melody in measures 3 - 4 and 8 - 9.

75 Row, Row, Row Your Boat

Folk

Additional: TRANSPOSE **Row, Row, Row Your Boat** to D♭ major.

119

I, IV, and V⁷ Chords

Identify the I, IV, and V^7 chords in *BIG ROCK CANDY MOUNTAIN* and *JOLLY GOOD FELLOW* then practice each piece.

76 BIG ROCK CANDY MOUNTAIN

Shift R.H. 2 up to A.

Folk

Oh the buz-zing of the bees in the lol - li - pop trees by the

Shift to R.H. 5 to A.

so - da wa - ter foun - tain, And the le - mon-ade springs where the

blue - bird sings, On the Big Rock Can - dy Moun - tain.

D. C. al Fine (or "Da Capo al Fine"): Go back to the beginning and repeat to the measure marked "Fine" (end).

77 JOLLY GOOD FELLOW

Folk

For he's a Jol-ly good fel-low, for he's a Jol-ly good

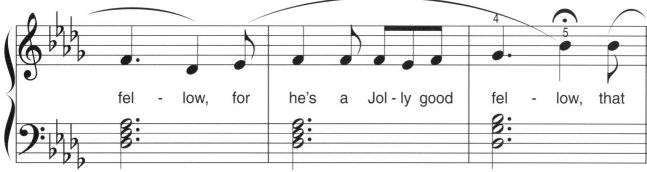

fel - low, for he's a Jol-ly good fel - low, that

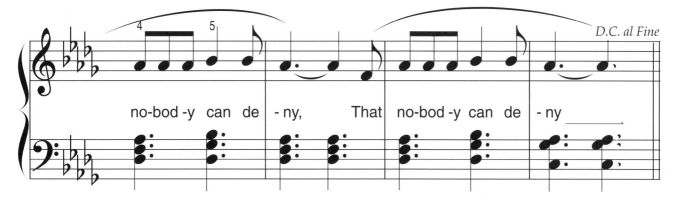

no-bod-y can de - ny_____. That

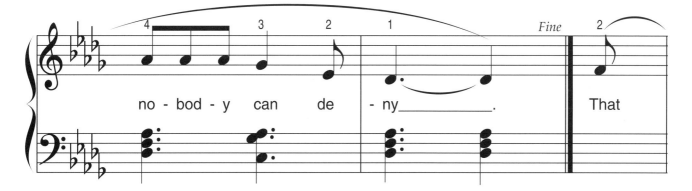

no-bod-y can de - ny, That no-bod-y can de - ny _____

Notice how intervals as well as chords form the accompaniment in *JINGLE BELLS.*

78 JINGLE BELLS

Pierpont

Dash-ing thro' the snow in a one horse o - pen sleigh,

O'er the fields we go, Laugh-ing all the way;

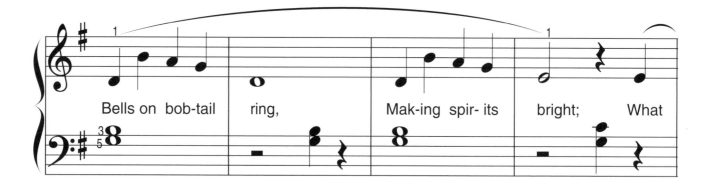

Bells on bob-tail ring, Mak-ing spir- its bright; What

fun it is to ride and sing A sleigh-ing song to - night! Oh,

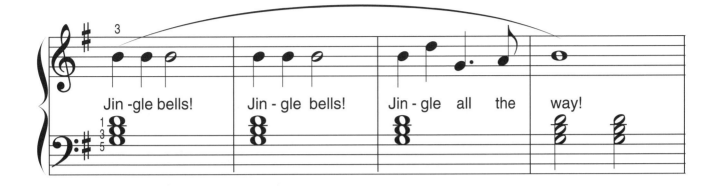

Jin -gle bells! Jin - gle bells! Jin - gle all the way!

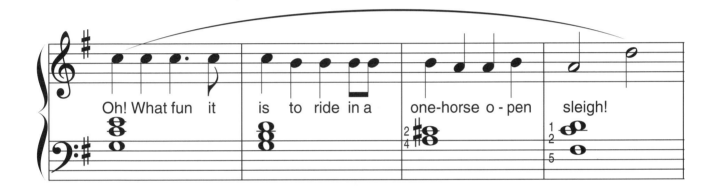

Oh! What fun it is to ride in a one-horse o - pen sleigh!

Jin -gle bells! Jin - gle bells! Jin - gle all the way!

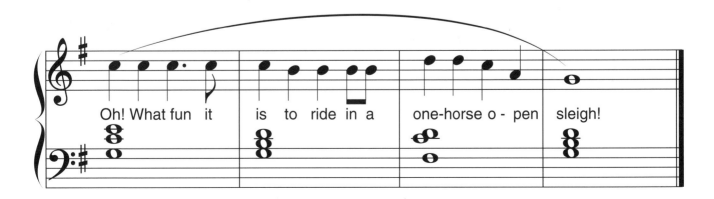

Oh! What fun it is to ride in a one-horse o - pen sleigh!

123

Minor i and iv Chords

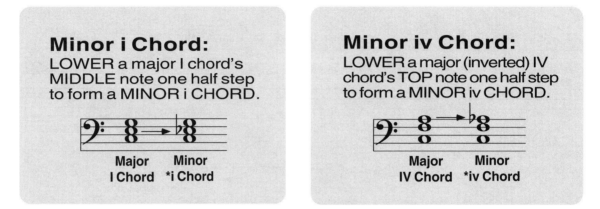

Minor i Chord:
LOWER a major I chord's MIDDLE note one half step to form a MINOR i CHORD.

Major I Chord   Minor *i Chord

Minor iv Chord:
LOWER a major (inverted) IV chord's TOP note one half step to form a MINOR iv CHORD.

Major IV Chord   Minor *iv Chord

*Minor chords are often indicated with lower case letters and numbers.

Learn to play the i-iv-i chord progression as written below. Then, transpose the i-iv-i chords to the remaining keys of e, f, f♯, g, a♭, a, b♭ and b minor. Practice *SWAN LAKE* (page 125), an example of music harmonized with i and iv chords.

79 I-IV-I CHORD PROGRESSION

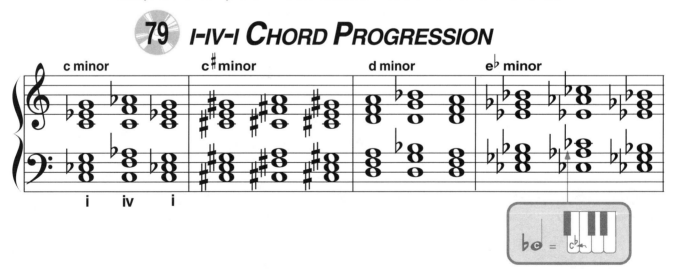

80 SWAN LAKE

Tchaikowsky

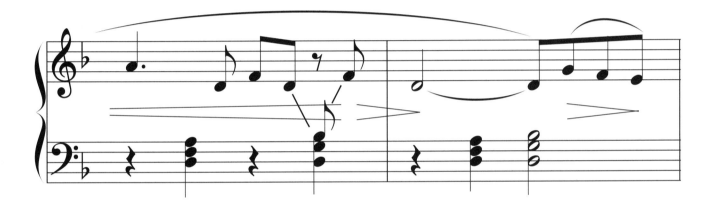

Count: "1 & 2 & 3 & 4 &"

Ritardando (rit.): gradually slow down.

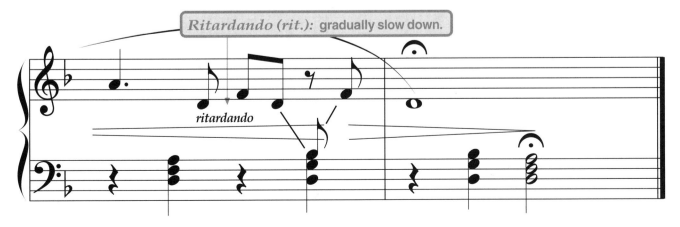

ritardando

2364

DANCE uses a minor i chord and the V⁷ chord you already know—V⁷ chords are the same for both major and minor keys. Clap and count aloud the rhythm of the melody in *DANCE.* Next, clap and count the rhythm of the chord accompaniment. Play hands alone and then together.

81 *DANCE*

Israeli

Alternate V⁷ Chords

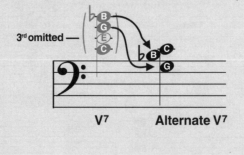

Sometimes, an ALTERNATE V⁷ CHORD is used, as in the last line of *DAYEYNU* (next page). This alternate V⁷ omits the third tone of a complete V⁷

126

Practice the chords and the melody alone, then play *DAYENU,* following the indicated fingering.

82 **DAYEYNU**

Folk Song

Practice *Skater's Waltz* hands alone then hands together. Notice how the melody in measures 1 - 4 repeats as a sequence in measures 5 - 8.

83 *Skater's Waltz*

128

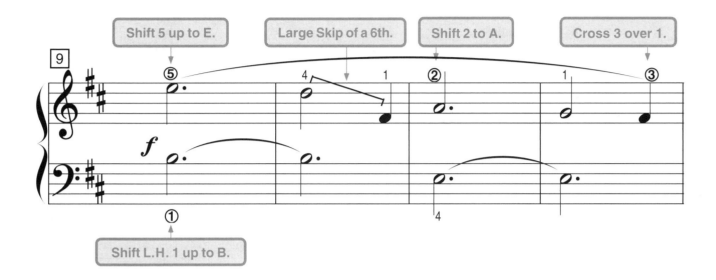

Shift 5 up to E.

Large Skip of a 6th.

Shift 2 to A.

Cross 3 over 1.

Shift L.H. 1 up to B.

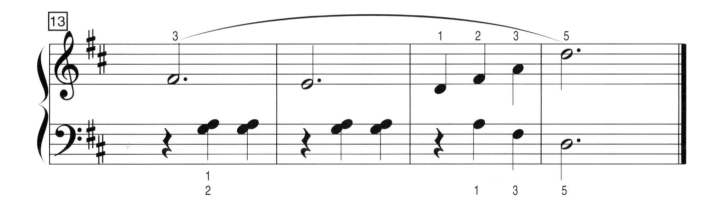

Binary Compositions

Binary (AB) Compositions:

In longer compositions, two or more phrases often create larger units or SECTIONS. Music composed of two sections (called an "A section" and a "B section") forms a BINARY, or two-part, "A-B" composition.

As you practice *CHIAPANECAS,* listen to the contrast between the A and B sections.

84 CHIAPANECAS

Mexican

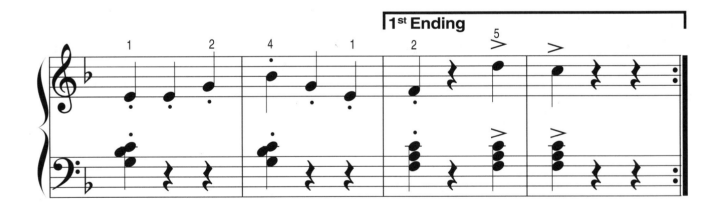

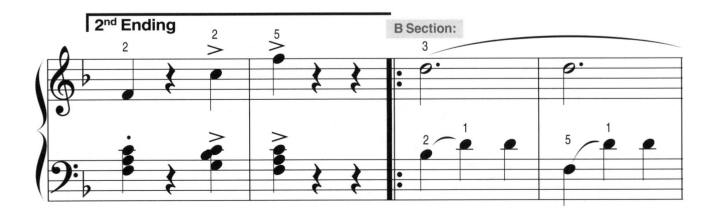

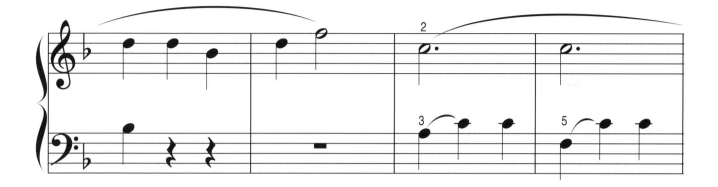

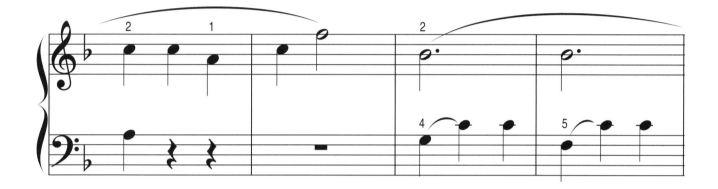

1st Ending

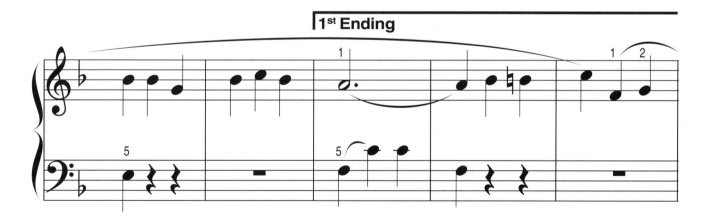

2nd Ending

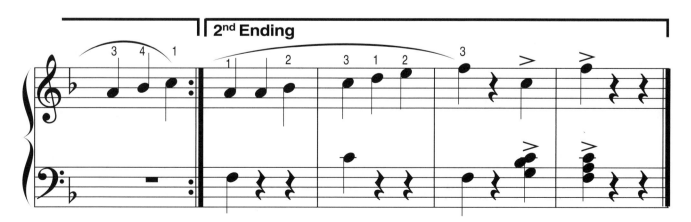

2364

In *GREENSLEEVES,* new material in measures 17 - 18 seems to introduce a contrasting B Section. However, except for measures 17 - 18 and 25 - 26, "Section B" actually repeats Section A exactly.

85 GREENSLEEVES

English Folk Song

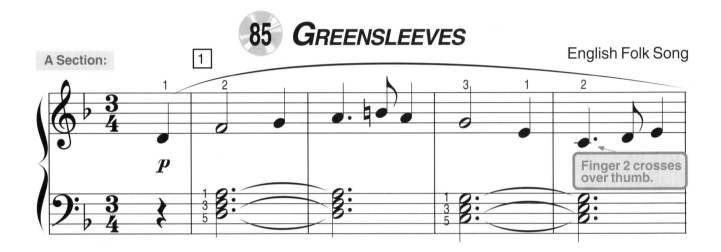

Finger 2 crosses over thumb.

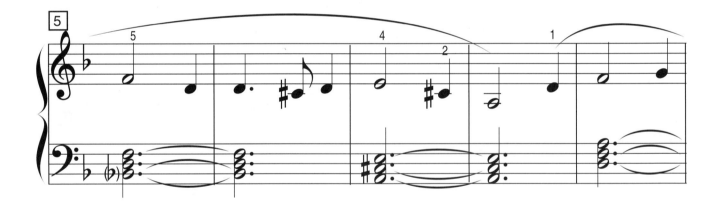

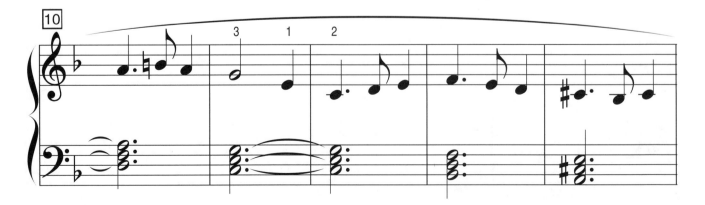

B Section:

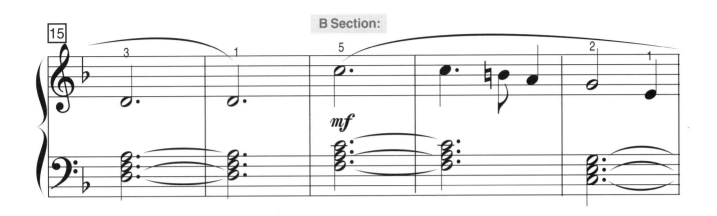

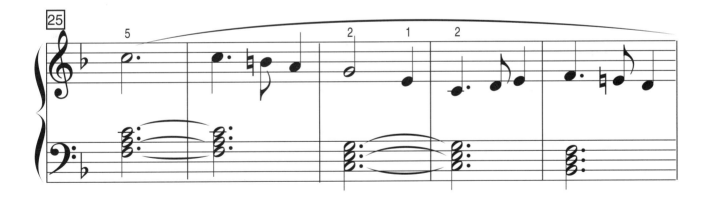

1st Ending **2nd Ending**

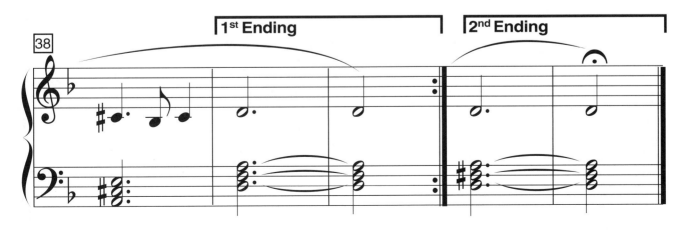

2364

The A and B sections in *GERMAN DANCE* contrast with one another. Notice, however, that the two sections are also similar in some ways.

86 GERMAN DANCE

Audio: Repeat Omitted

Haydn

A Section:

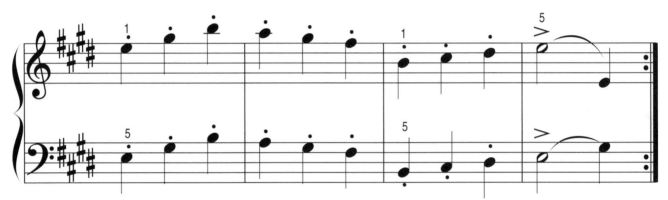

B Section:

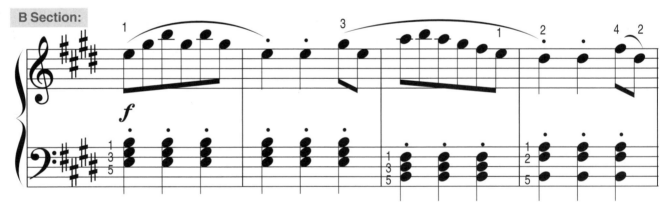

2364

The Damper Pedal

This sign ⌐____⌐ means use the DAMPER pedal. The damper pedal (the right-most pedal) sustains tones. It raises the felt dampers off the strings inside the piano, allowing them to vibrate freely. Press down the damper pedal with the ball of your right foot. Keep your heel on the floor.

Press Down   **Release**
└──────────── **Hold** ────────────┘

Pedal as you play these half notes. Say "down" and "up" as you pedal. (Hint: Wait until you actually HEAR the next tone, then lift the the pedal and press it down again.)

Down   Up Down Up Down *etc.*

PEDAL ETUDE is composed of broken, or ARPEGGIATED, chords. Practice *PEDAL ETUDE* a few times without pedaling then add the pedal. Notice that your right hand plays in the bass clef in measures 5 - 8.

PEDAL ETUDE 87

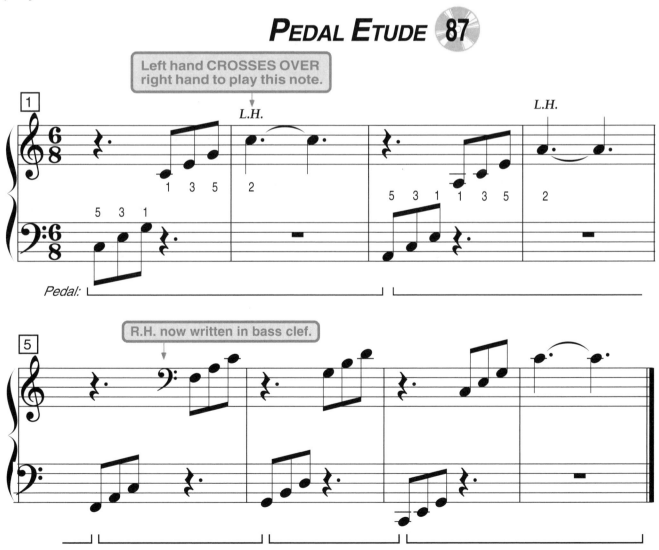

Syncopation:

SYNCOPATION occurs when a normally "WEAK"* main beat is ACCENTED, or, when a beat BETWEEN main beats is ACCENTED.

Rest on beat "3" plus quarter note on beat "4" moves accent from "strong" third beat to "weak" fourth beat.

Eighth note tied to quarter note creates accent in between main beats.

*The first beat of a measure is normally the strongest beat, receiving more emphasis than the others. Beats that follow the first beat are generally weaker. In $\frac{2}{4}$ and $\frac{3}{4}$ time, beat "1" is strongest. The other beats are weaker. In $\frac{4}{4}$ time, beat "1" is strongest while beat "3" is next strongest. Beats "2" and "4" are weakest.

Clap the rhythm of the melody in *THAT SYNCHIN' FEELIN'*. Notice the syncopation in measures 2, 3 - 4, 6, and 7 - 8. Clap the rhythm of the left hand. Observe that the V⁷ chords in this part move downward by half steps in measures 3 and 5. In measure 7, the left hand plays intervals of a 5ᵗʰ while the right hand plays 4ᵗʰs. These combined intervals form a new chord sound. Practice *THAT SYNCHIN' FEELIN'* hands separately, then hands together.

 **88** *THAT SYNCHIN' FEELIN'*

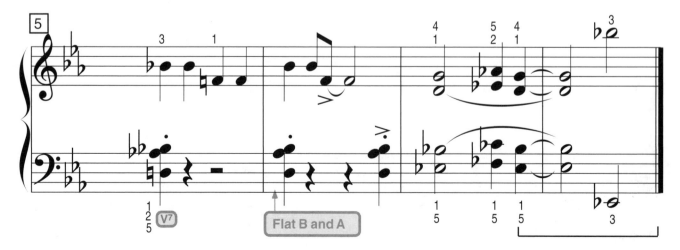

136

ERIE BLUES, a variation on **ERIE CANAL** (page 84), uses the tones of a C blues scale—
C, E♭, F, F♯(G♭) and G. Clap the rhythm of **ERIE BLUES**, listening for syncopation.
Practice hands separately, then hands together. Notice that your right hand
moves to the treble clef in measure 7.

ERIE BLUES

With "Jazzy"
Rhythmic Freedom

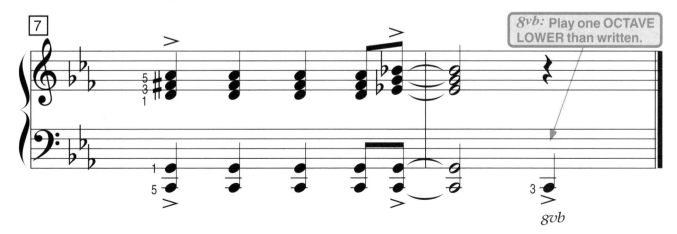

8vb: **Play one OCTAVE
LOWER than written.**

8vb

137

Playing Octaves

In **DARK EYES,** octaves in your left hand add fullness to the accompaniment. These octaves move upward in a stepwise progression. Notice that the top note of each left hand octave forms the bottom note of the suceeding chord, in measures 1 - 5.

1 Identify the i, iv, and V^7 chords in the accompaniment. Play your left hand alone then practice it while pedaling.

2 Play your right hand alone, observing the indicated fingering.

3 Play hands together without pedaling. Balance the sound of your right and left hands so that the melody is heard clearly. Follow the indicated dynamic markings. Add the pedal.

90 DARK EYES

Russian

Passionately. With Rhythmic Flexibility, or "Rubato."

OCTAVE HIGHER than written.

8va --
(optional)

8vb⌐ (optional)

OCTAVE LOWER than written.

Look for repetitions and sequences in the melody of *EASY WINNERS.* Identify I, IV and V⁷ chords in the accompaniment. Practice hands alone and then together.

91 *THE EASY WINNERS*

Scott Joplin

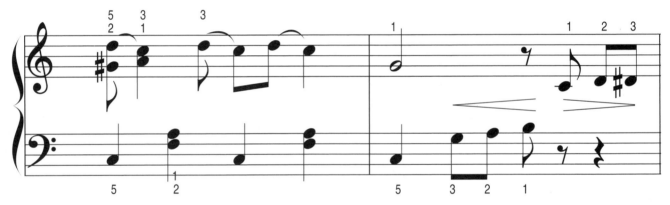

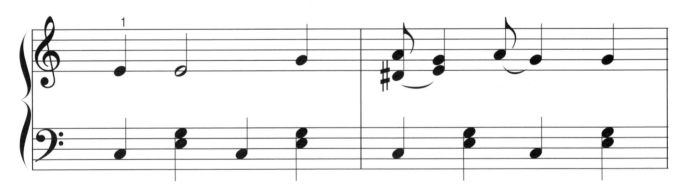

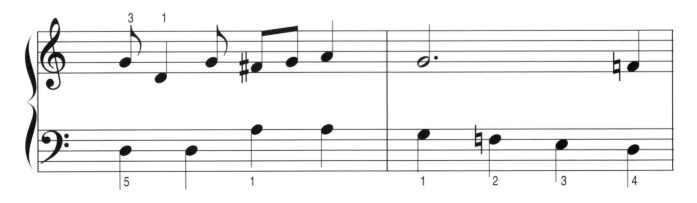

2364

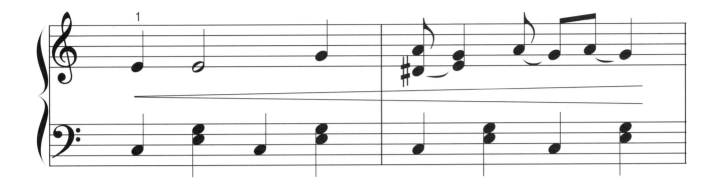

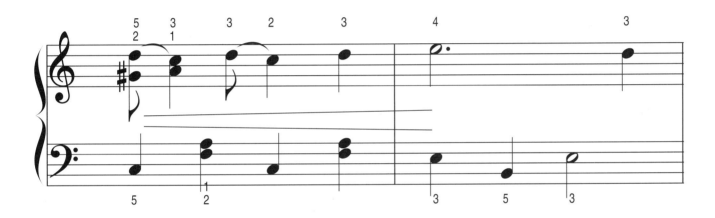

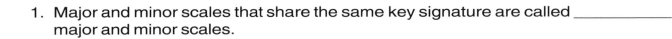

Review
(Pages 74 -141)

1. Major and minor scales that share the same key signature are called _____ major and minor scales.

2. To make a minor i chord, lower the _____note of a root position major chord.

3. A relative minor key's name is found one _____ below the letter name of the major key signature.
   (step or skip)

4. Write the major and minor names for these key signatures.

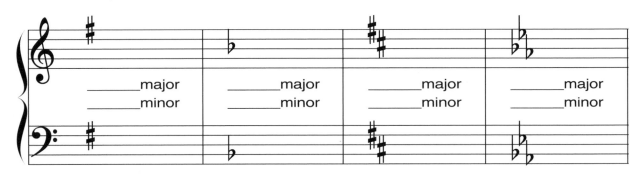

_____major
_____minor

_____major
_____minor

_____major
_____minor

_____major
_____minor

5. In the blanks, write the letter of the term that matches each definition.

   A. Ostinato   ___Lowers pitch one half step

   B. Crescendo   ___Cancels preceding flat or sharp

   C. Sequence   ___Slow down gradually

   D. Ritardando ___Raises pitch one half step.

   E. ♮   ___Melodic pattern that recurs on different notes

   F. ♭   ___Get loud gradually

   G. ♯   ___Accompaniment figure that repeats over and over

6. Write in the BARLINES for this rhythmic pattern so that four beats occur in each measure. Clap this rhythm while counting aloud.

2364

7. Write the IV chords for these major I chords.

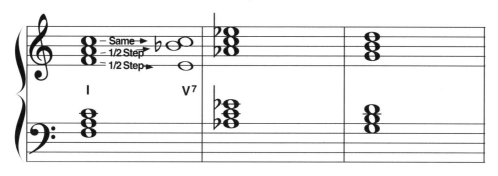

8. Write the V⁷ for these major I chords.

9. **Composing and Improvising:** Review the various ways of improvising and composing we studied on pages 7, 18, 59, 63, 69, 70, 95, 97, 102 - 103, and 113.

    Extra: Try additional ways of improvising or composing that you may think of.

Congratulations!
You have completed
PIANO—PLAIN AND
SIMPLE! VOLUME I.

Glossary

Accent ($\downarrow$): symbol over or under note indicating to play markedly, with emphasis.

Allegro: quickly.

Allegretto: moderately quickly.

Andante: at a walking tempo.

Common time (c): $\frac{4}{4}$ time.

Crescendo (*cresc.* or ⟨⟩): get louder gradually.

Da capo al fine *(D.C. al fine)*: repeat from beginning up to indication of *"fine"* (end).

Decrescendo (*decresc.* or ⟩): get softer gradually.

Fermata (⌢): hold note longer than its regular value.

Flat ($\flat$): indicates that a pitch is to be lowered one half-step.

Forte (*f*): loud.

Fortissimo (*ff*): very loud.

Half Step: two adjacent tones with no other tone between.

Legato: smoothly.

Mezzo Forte (*mf*): medium loud.

Mezzo Piano (*mp*): medium soft.

Natural ($\natural$): cancels flats or sharps previously applied to a pitch.

8va: 8va above a note means play one octave higher than written.

Pianissimo (*pp*): very soft.

Piano (*p*): soft.

Ritardando (*rit.*): gradually slow down.

Sharp ($\sharp$): indicates that a pitch is to be raised one half step.

Slur (⌢): curved line above or below two or more different notes. indicates notes should be played smoothly.

Staccato ($\dot\downarrow$): dot above or below a note. Note is to be played in short, detached manner.

Tempo: rate of speed at which piece is played.

Tie (⌣): curved line between two or more consecutive notes of the same pitch. play and hold the first note for the total value of all notes in a tied group.

Whole Step: two tones separated by one other tone between them.